SPICER AND PEGLER'S

THE BUSINESS OF PARTNERSHIPS

AUSTRALIA AND NEW ZEALAND
The Law Book Company Ltd.
Sydney : Melbourne : Perth

CANADA AND U.S.A.
The Carswell Company Ltd.
Agincourt, Ontario

INDIA
N.M. Tripathi Private Ltd.
Bombay
and
Eastern Law House Private Ltd.
Calcutta and Delhi
M.P.P. House
Bangalore

ISRAEL
Steimatzky's Agency Ltd.
Jerusalem : Tel Aviv : Haifa

MALAYSIA : SINGAPORE : BRUNEI
Malayan Law Journal (Pte.) Ltd.
Singapore and Kuala Lumpur

PAKISTAN
Pakistan Law House
Karachi

SPICER AND PEGLER'S

THE BUSINESS OF PARTNERSHIPS

by

Peter J. Oliver, F.C.A

and

Nigel T. Davey, M.A., F.C.A.

LONDON
Sweet & Maxwell
1986

Published by
Sweet & Maxwell Limited of
11 New Fetter Lane, London,
Computerset by Promenade Graphics Limited, Cheltenham.

Printed in Scotland
Reprinted 1987

British Library Cataloguing in Publication Data

Oliver, Peter
Spicer and Pegler's The business of
partnerships.
1. Partnerships—Great Britain
I. Title   II. Davey, Nigel   III. Spicer,
Pegler
338.7'3'0941   KD2051

ISBN 0–421–35330–9

Introduction

This book is directed at all partners in a professional partnership, and at those who, while not necessarily partners, are engaged in the management of a partnership. It presents the advice that we have found our partnership clients ask for as they face the problems not only of practising their professions but of running successful businesses. There are those who still argue that all that is necessary for success in such a field is the provision of a professional service of the highest quality. That, the argument goes, will lead to a successful business. That may still be true for a minority of firms in a special position, but even for those, we believe that the time is fast approaching when they will have to view their firms as businesses and manage them accordingly. For a partnership, that presents particular problems and it has been our aim to identify those problems and some of the ways they may be tackled. While the detailed solution to a given problem will vary from firm to firm, it has been our experience that the principles of both the problem and the solution are remarkably constant whatever the size of the partnership. We believe, therefore, that what we have written has application to firms of all sizes. At the present time, many firms are contemplating incorporation and, frequently, the involvement of outside investors. We foresee that trend continuing but we did not consider this book to be the appropriate medium for discussing the problems of transition from partnership to a company. We believe, however, that many of the subjects addressed in this book, particularly those concerned with business organisation and management, will have equal application whether the profession is conducted through a partnership or a company.

On a point of detail, we must explain the lack of any reference in the book to even the possibility of ladies being partners. Our reason is the practical one that it is easier simply to use the masculine gender. We hope this is acceptable to the lady partners in our own firm and elsewhere.

This is not a textbook. If detailed guidance is required on a tax point, or on how to structure a ledger so that it gives the required information, readers must look elsewhere. What we hope they will gain from this book is an understanding of some of the problems peculiar to the professional partnership and the approach to their solution, whether the reader be a partner about to retire, a new partner just joining the practice, or the managing or finance partner with specific management responsibilities.

PJO
NTD

Friary Court
London EC3N 2NP
January 1986

Acknowledgements

In many ways this book owes its existence to Eddie Ray. He not only introduced us to the fascinating subject of advising partnerships, but taught us a great deal of what we now know about them and also found the time to read and comment critically on a final draft of this book. Many of our other partners too, wittingly or not, have helped us, if only by discussing the problems that form the subject of this book, but we must mention particularly Rob Beard and Bob Willott both of whom contributed materially by commenting on early drafts of several chapters. We have also been greatly assisted by William Barnes who drafted many of the appendices and provided much useful comment. We thank all of them and also our partnership clients for the opportunities they have given us over the years to develop our thinking by discussing with them their own partnership problems.

Acknowledgements

Contents

ix

1 Organisation and Structure

It is perhaps only a slight exaggeration to claim that the biggest problem of running a partnership, especially a professional partnership, is the partners themselves! If there is more than a grain of truth in this, why should it be so? The answer lies partly in the inherent unsuitability of partnership as a form of business organisation and partly in the fact that individuals have been attracted to form or join partnerships primarily because they wish to practice their particular profession. If they have thought about it at all at the time of joining a partnership, any aspirations as to running the partnership as a business are almost always of only slight significance for the average new partner. Indeed, even if the existing partners are alive to the needs of viewing their practice as a business, they are likely to appoint new partners for their perceived abilities as practitioners rather than as business men as such. For almost all partners, therefore, the idea that they have to regard their practice as anything other than a profession represents a change of attitude for them. Some partners make the change quickly, others never at all. Indeed some would argue that the provision of the particular professional service at a high level of competence is the only requirement of a partner and that all other matters of a business nature are secondary. If the level of service is appropriate, it is argued, everything else will follow automatically. That is not a counsel we would support. In a market where the particular profession's services are in short supply, it might prove successful for a time, even over a number of years. But we believe that the combination of an ever-more competitive environment for professions just as much as for other businesses and the strains inherent in the partnership concept will, sooner or later, require any firm if it is to prosper, to come to terms with the fact that it must view itself as a business and organise itself accordingly. That is not to say that it should in any way ignore the need for professional excellence. Clearly no firm will survive if it does so. It is merely to recognise that the maintenance of that professional excellence at an appropriate level is but one requirement for run-

ning the partnership successfully. Most partners will have no difficulty in agreeing that it is no good enjoying giving an excellent professional service if it does not provide an adequate financial
reward. A professional firm can no longer assume that the one will
continue automatically to flow from the other.

Proprietorship and Executive Control

Admission as an equity partner confers certain proprietorial
rights. Not only is the partner now responsible for the proper professional conduct of his clients' affairs solely to the firm (his fellow
partners), but he has a right to a part of the net assets of the firm
(represented by his capital and drawings accounts), a right to a
defined share of the firm's profits and the ability to commit and be
committed by his fellow partners, both professionally and financially. His position is, in many ways analogous to that of a shareholder and, at any rate in larger partnerships, to that of a minority
shareholder. The important difference is that he, and all the other
"shareholders", have a direct responsibility for how the firm performs professionally and financially. Whatever the partner's
declared attitude to viewing the practice as a business he is thus
likely to expect to play some part in the decision taking process of
the firm, whereas a minority shareholder will expect to delegate
that responsibility to a board of directors.

For a small partnership, up to say four or five equity partners,
there may be little difficulty, in practice, in meeting the needs of
the proprietors (the partners) to be fully involved in the business.
Both strategic decisions (moving offices, opening a new office,
moving into a new sphere of business) and minor day to day matters (what salary increase should the secretaries be awarded,
should the firm buy another word processor) can be dealt with at
regular partners' meetings. Those meetings thus serve the dual
function of a shareholders' meeting and a meeting of the board of
directors.

Even in a small firm, however, and perhaps not even as a con-
scious business decision, some executive decisions are likely to be
delegated to a single partner. The word "delegate" may not always
appear to be the correct one. The senior partner may simply take
some decisions without reference to his partners, merely reporting
to them afterwards what he has done. But what has actually happened is that the rights of the other partners to participate in those
particular decisions have been delegated to the single partner who
is thereby responsible to the partnership as a whole for his actions.

If he makes a mess of it he can expect the other partners to withdraw that delegation and pass it to another of their number.

As firms grow such delegation is forced upon the partnership simply because there is not the time, or in the case of some partners the inclination, for everyone to get deeply involved in running the business. But if this greater delegation is to lead to efficiency in the running of the firm, some detailed thought must be given to precisely what is to be delegated and how lines of responsibility and communication between partners are to be defined. To return to the analogy of the company; the shareholders will expect there to be a chairman and a board of directors, possibly a managing director and perhaps also one or more committees of the board to deal with particular aspects of the business. A partnership must decide what form of structure it needs to enable it to meet the twin objectives of providing a competent professional service to its clients and providing a reasonable living for its partners (and indeed its staff).

An Organisational Structure

It must be said at this point, and it will be repeated throughout this book, that each partnership must work out what suits it best. A partnership is no more than a collection of individuals and each partnership will build up, over the years, certain attitudes to business and professional matters which will be different from any other partnership. The organisation most appropriate for it is therefore unlikely to be appropriate, in all its details, for any other firm. But, as with so many features of partnership, the basic principles are common to most firms and the form of organisation outlined below is capable of adaptation to meet most firms' needs.

Senior Partner, Managing Partner

It is often the case that an organisation, business or otherwise, and regardless of its size, is more likely to be successful if it is under the direction of a single personality who is widely accepted within the organisation as its leader. In other words, in the context of a partnership, a high degree of executive authority is delegated to such a person by the other partners. Within any existing successful partnership there is, therefore, quite likely to be such a partner in place, whatever the formal structure of the firm. He may be the senior partner (though seniority in terms of age or length of service does not necessarily imply that such a person has the other qualities required for leadership) or he may be a less senior partner. The functions of such a leading partner are analogous to that of both the chairman of the board of the company and the managing director, and just as the two functions may be fulfilled by the same director or two different directors so they may be split in partnerships. Often the two functions will be performed by the senior partner, but, especially in larger firms, there will be a separate managing or executive partner. In that event the role of the senior partner is usually to chair partners' meetings, and to act as the firm's leading representative to the world at large. He will, ideally, also act as a foil to the managing partner and as someone to whom any other partner can turn to for advice or a second opinion on matters affecting partners individually.

Executive Committee

Once a firm grows to the size of 15 or 20 partners, it is likely that the efficient running of the business and the desire of most or all partners to spend a significant amount of their time on client matters will demand that the executive responsibilities of the firm be shared by a number of partners forming an executive or management committee. Such a committee should be chaired by the managing partner, or by the senior partner if he also fulfils the managing partner role.

Executive Action

The executive function within a partnership may thus be fulfilled principally by one man (the managing partner, who may also be the senior partner) or by the managing partner and a number of other partners forming an executive committee. What types of executive action should be delegated by the other partners to the managing partner or the executive committee? Once again this is a matter that must be thought about and developed by each firm to suit its own requirements, but it is likely to include some or all of the following:

Professional matters:

— ensuring that there is a proper mechanism for monitoring and maintaining the quality of the firm's professional advice. Normally the executive would not itself be the means of monitoring standards; its responsibility would be to ensure that there was an effective organisation in the firm to meet that requirement. That organisation would involve other partners (but need not necessarily exclude a partner just because he is also a member of the executive). It would also embrace staff and partner training.

Business matters:

— developing and updating a business plan for the approval of the whole partnership. This plan will embrace the development of existing services, investigation of new services or business areas to be explored, extension into new geographical areas and withdrawal from specific business or geographical areas;

— approval of annual financial budgets. This will require approval of the underlying business assumptions built into the budgets, for example fee and salary rates and personnel numbers;

— monitoring of actual performance against budget and taking any necessary management action to correct deviations from that budget;

— identifying likely needs for future partners and determining broad personnel policies;

— efficient operation and utilisation of the office facilities, *e.g.* computers, word processors, telephones and other communications facilities, library.

The division of these functions between the managing or senior partner and the executive must be determined by each firm; there can be no hard and fast rules. In addition to the foregoing, however, it is usually appropriate for the senior or managing partner to have the authority to re-allocate work amongst partners where that is necessary and to deal with complaints made to the firm. The question of re-allocation of work between partners can be an emotive one but, in most firms, situations develop where some partners take on more than they can cope with. In that event it is in the interest of both that partner and the firm as a whole that he should be relieved of some of his client or administrative work as appropriate and that this be taken on by other partners.

It is common to find that some of the above functions are delegated to separate committees or individual partners. Thus in larger firms one commonly finds separate committees or individual partners responsible for finance, administration and personnel and sometimes also a practice development committee which is responsible for the planning matters outlined above. In medium sized practices such committees may report direct to the partnership as a whole without reporting through an executive committee.

Provided there is a sufficiently small number of partners (certainly no more than 20) to enable full partners' meetings to debate properly recommendations put forward by those committees and to take the necessary decisions, that may be a perfectly workable and practical approach. But once a partnership increases to the level where there are too many partners to debate properly individual issues it becomes essential to operate through an executive committee which should consist of no more than five or six partners so that proper review and debate is possible. It is essential that minutes are kept by the executive committee and circulated to all partners who are thereby kept fully aware of matters being discussed and decisions taken by the executive.

Choosing the Executive

There are no rules for choosing the managing partner and not many for choosing the executive! Some firms, particularly very large ones, formally elect a managing partner or a senior partner but for the vast majority of medium sized firms it is a matter of personalities, lobbying and consensus. The fact that there may be no formality in the process need not matter. The important thing is that partners must have confidence in whoever is appointed. Once the partnership loses that confidence it had better find a new man.

There are three common ways of choosing an executive committee. Members can be selected by the senior partner or managing partner, they can be elected by all the partners, or they can be chosen to represent specific departments or offices of the firm. While the departmental or office representative method is commonly used, it suffers from the sometimes severe disadvantage that the committee members may be concerned first to look after the interests of those they represent and less about the firm as a whole. If they are elected or simply appointed there is a better chance that they will think first of the firm as a whole. Apart from that factor, the method used is largely a matter of personal preference of the partners.

Professional Administrators

As partnerships develop, the view is commonly expressed by partners that they would like to avoid the burdens and responsibilities of managing the firm by devolving those responsibilities on to a professional administrator, perhaps a partnership secretary who may also be a qualified accountant. Provided it is recognised that the responsibilities of a partner, as a partner, cannot be wholly delegated, this is a sensible route; but it is essential that a single partner (if there is a relevant committee, perhaps the chairman of that committee) retains the ultimate responsibility to the partnership for whatever matters are delegated to a partnership secretary or other professional manager.

The two most common areas for such delegation are finance and administration. If not included within administration, personnel is also often recognised as a separate function for delegation. The degree of delegation and the level of expertise of the manager appointed must depend very much on the size of the firm. A substantial firm probably has the need for separate managers for each function whereas a smaller firm will not have the same need or be able to justify the expense of two or three separate managers. The roles of finance and administration are often successfully combined in one person as are administration and personnel, but the firm which can find a single person with the necessary skills in all these areas is lucky indeed. The definition of the post to be filled must therefore be carefully drawn and the firm must determine which aspects warrant the greatest priority if the skills of the applicants for such a job are to be successfully matched to the firm's needs.

Departmental Structure

Even small firms tend to divide themselves into departments for the purpose of providing the relevant professional service in the most efficient manner. This may come about because a particular partner, and the staff most often working with him, come to specialise in some particular aspect of professional work or because the practice is conducted through a number of offices which thereby become, effectively, separate departments. In larger firms division into departments is likely to be essential from an operational point of view. Often it will be an essential means of developing and maintaining expertise in a particular field of the profession. For example, a firm of solicitor's may wish, for that reason, to handle all its litigation work through a single department specialising in that work, or a surveyor may have a separate rating department. Even in a general practice where all partners turn their hands to all matters within their professional expertise, size may dictate some divisionalisation simply so that the work of the staff can be allocated and controlled effectively. Such control is more likely to be achieved amongst a smaller grouping of people than amongst a larger group. The nature of the work, the total size of the firm and the style of management will all influence the optimum size of a working group within any particular firm so it is not possible to give general guidance.

Once a departmental structure emerges, its relationship to the overall management structure of the firm must be considered. The departments having been set up for reasons of professional administration and practice, they can also be used as profit centres for measuring the profitability of the particular type of work being carried out. Alternatively they can be used as cost centres simply for the purpose of controlling costs. But if either of those routes is followed and the partners in those departments become responsible for the financial performance of their departments they will need to be represented on whatever part of the executive function of the firm (the executive committee or the finance committee) is responsible for approving budgets and monitoring financial performance. It will also be essential that the levels of authority of the committees and executive partners are clearly established and understood.

The route followed is likely to be determined partly by the nature of the divisionalisation. If each department represents a separate geographical office, it is almost inevitable that it will assume a financial as well as an organisational responsibility. This will also be likely if the division reflects significantly different types of business within the firm; partners are likely to want to know whether each category of business is profitable. The route must, however, be followed with care, for in many businesses the work done by one department for a client can be a necessary pre-requisite for obtaining other work from that client and a direct comparison of profitability without regard to such other factors could be misleading. Thus a firm of commercial property surveyors may deal in domestic property solely as a service to directors of client companies and not make a full charge for such work. If, however, departments have been created merely for administrative convenience and they do not reflect differing activities or locations, it is less likely that they will also be used as the basis for financial responsibility.

Parallel Partnerships

Parallel partnerships have two purposes. They can be used as a mechanism for overcoming a tax problem on a merger, as explained in Chapter 16, and they can be used to bring into partnership those who are not suitably professionally qualified so as to be admitted to the main partnership; that is the subject of this section.

The trend today is for each profession to extend the boundaries of its traditional activities. As a result firms frequently find themselves employing members of other professions and, sooner or later, if those new areas of activity prosper, they will wish to appoint some of those other professionals to principal status. Equally they may wish to do the same for the professional administrators—the partnership secretary or partnership accountant. Quite apart from the question of status, the appointment to partnership confers on the individual significant tax advantages compared with a senior employee (see Chapter 8). Yet the rules of the relevant professional bodies normally prohibit the appointment as partners of those who are not members of that body. The solution can be the formation of a parallel partnership consisting of these other professionals and (except in the case of solicitors, where it is prohibited) a number of partners in the main firm.

Such a parallel partnership need have no organisational function in the business, though from a tax point of view it is necessary for it to be dealing with a discrete and recognisably separate aspect of the total firm's activity. The detailed arrangements must be tailored to the particular requirements of the firm and the constraints imposed by its professional body. Both aspects must be examined carefully with appropriate professional advice before embarking on the establishment of such a partnership.

Development of Partners

All too often, appointment of a senior member of staff to partnership is seen at the time as the pinnacle of an individual's achievement; all parties breath a sigh of relief and it is assumed that the new partner will fit into the partnership and all will be well. But partners, like staff, benefit from training and the well organised firm will have in place a programme for training partners not only to keep them up to date in technical professional matters but also for developing them as individual partners. Such a development programme will involve an explanation to the new partner of the partnership structure and the role expected now and in the future from him in relation to the running of the firm's own business. At least for the first few years of partnership, a periodic review with the senior or managing partner of the younger partner's professional development can also be helpful. If the partner has been admitted on a probationary basis for the first few years, such a review is essential. But in any case, it may provide an opportunity to encourage him to pursue a particular line of professional specialisation, or ensure that if he has, for example, administrative ability, this is put to best use in the running of the firm without causing an undue conflict with his desire to concentrate on client work. If a partner is to become involved with the management of the firm, he will probably benefit from specific training in the skills of management. Similarly, since all partners must, to some extent be salesmen, and since many find the concept of selling an uncomfortable bedfellow to the practising of a profession, partners will also benefit from training in the basic skills of marketing and selling. The matters of concern to the person about to become a partner are dealt with in Chapter 14.

The partner approaching retirement must not be overlooked. The age at which a partner will wish to work less hard will vary from person to person and some will not wish to slow down before they retire. But it is important that the wishes of partners in this respect are established and that proper steps are taken to prepare for any reduced workload or for the orderly transfer of client responsibilities from those who wish to be kept fully in harness to the day they retire. Failure to do this can jeopardise the firm's goodwill with its clients.

The Partnership Agreement

This chapter began, deliberately, with a discussion of the partnership as a business rather than with a discussion of the legal basis and implications of partnerships. An understanding of the partnership as a business is vital to the successful development of the firm in a competitive commercial environment. But the legal basis cannot be ignored. It may give rise to some of the problems that have been discussed earlier in this chapter but it also provides the framework on which the organisation of the firm must be based. Like many other legal agreements, a partnership agreement does not need to be written down; an oral agreement is just as enforceable. However, the obvious difficulty with an unwritten agreement is establishing precisely what has been agreed. A formal, written partnership agreement is therefore strongly recommended. It should be reasonably comprehensive so that partners know where they stand on all the areas that affect the conduct of the partnership. Commonly, a formal agreement will be drawn up only periodically, with supplemental agreements being entered into to take account of changes in the composition of the partnership and shares of profit, thereby admitting new partners to the agreement or releasing retiring partners from its obligations. Important partnership decisions can effectively be grafted on to a partnership agreement by means of a partnership minute which is signed by all the partners. This will have the same legal effect as a supplemental agreement. It will be found, for example, that changes in the profit sharing arrangements will frequently be dealt with in this manner rather than by completely redrawing the partnership agreement. After a while, however, an agreement which has been subsequently amended and added to by supplemental agreements and partnership minutes can become unwieldy (rather in the same way as does taxation legislation with the passing of successive Finance Acts) and a periodic consolidation and revision then becomes worthwhile.

In the absence of specific agreement between the partners, the partnership will be bound by the terms of the Partnership Act 1890 which specifies certain provisions for dealing with partnership profits, assets and conduct in specific areas. While the provisions of this Act are eminently reasonable and sensible, most firms will prefer to determine their own destiny and will want to agree between themselves how to deal with these important matters. Appendix 1 suggests the headings which will be appropriate for most partnership agreements and includes a brief discussion of the important aspects which might be covered by each section.

2 The Firm's Accounts

Financial accounting is merely the accountant's rather formal way of describing how a business's housekeeping records are maintained. Clearly a proper record must be kept of a firm's income and expenditure and of its assets and liabilities.

In this respect a partnership is no different from any other business enterprise and this chapter will not therefore describe the basic features of an accounting system; there are numerous books on that subject readily available. It concentrates therefore on those features of a system that are likely to require a modified approach to cater for the needs of a professional partnership.

While computers are an integral part of the management systems of most firms, it is not the purpose of this book to examine in detail what applications might most appropriately be computerised or, therefore, to explore, for particular applications the relative merits of micro, or mini-computer systems operated by the firm or the use of outside computer bureaux.

The Profit and Loss Account

Income

The income of most partnerships takes the form either of commission or of a fee. The crucial requirement is to ensure first that all work that should give rise to a fee does in fact do so and second that every fee raised is properly recorded (not least so that if it remains unpaid the client can be chased).

Ensuring that a fee is sent out for every job is not too difficult for a commission based business. Once an estate agent takes property off his register it is relatively simple to ensure that it is categorised either as a sale, and a corresponding entry made in a fee register, or as a non-sale with no further financial implications. The accounts department can then check, periodically, that all entries in the fee register have given rise to a fee. It is also relatively simple for a lawyer charging a fee on a conveyance to ensure that a fee is raised if, as is often the case with residential work, the fee is deducted from the sale proceeds or, in the case of a purchase, included in the solicitor's request for the client's funds to meet the purchase consideration. But it becomes much more difficult where the work being charged for is advice work. To ensure that all such work gives rise to an appropriate fee is one of the compelling reasons for maintaining work in progress records, usually on the basis of a time recording system as considered in the next chapter.

The second requirement identified above was to ensure that all fees rendered are properly recorded. In partnerships this can be particularly difficult as inevitably fees will be rendered by every partner, and perhaps by many senior fee earners as well; they will not, as in a manufacturing business, all be issued from one source within the organisation. If the partnership is small with perhaps only three or four people sending out fees, the invoices can be pre-numbered before they are issued to the secretaries who will type them. The accounts department can then easily check that each number is accounted for, provided of course, spoiled invoices are retained. But in most partnerships such a system would be impractical. A solution which is reasonably watertight and simple to operate is to instruct all those who type a fee to obtain the next sequential number from the accounts department and to type that number on the fee. Provided a check is made by the partner issuing the fee to see that a number does indeed appear on the invoice and the accounts department carry out a review of numbers as described above, this will give the desired result.

Once the fees have been rendered and, if necessary the client chased for payment, the next step is the receipt of cash. Much the same principles apply here as for other businesses, although in many cases the cheques may be received direct by partners in their personal mail. They cannot then be intercepted as part of any general mail opening procedure and immediately logged. There is no easy solution to this. The problem of the partner who receives a cheque and forgets to pass it on to the accounts department can only, ultimately, be dealt with when it appears that the partner's client has not paid his bill.

Disbursements

Almost all professional partnerships incur, on behalf of clients, expenditure that is recoverable from those clients. It is essential, therefore, that these are accurately recorded. This is a simple matter. Normally a separate disbursements ledger is maintained with an account for each client. For larger firms that also have a fully developed time recording system, the disbursements ledger can be linked to the time ledger so that when information about time spent is being sought preparatory to rendering a fee, any disbursements to be recovered are identified at the same time. Alternatively, where, as in the case of solicitors and estate agents, separate accounts are maintained for clients' monies held by the firm, the disbursement ledger can conveniently be linked to the clients' ledger. Many such disbursements are incurred by staff who commonly draw advances from the firm to fund such expenditure. Since that expenditure will ultimately be chargeable to clients many firms record those advances direct against the client disbursement account, crediting the client with any refund of the advance in excess of the actual expenditure. Whilst this may ensure that everything gets charged to the client it may not provide much discipline over staff and a better solution from that point of view is to record the advance against the staff member, making a transfer to the client only when the expenditure has actually been incurred and accounted for. Care must be taken in accounting for VAT. If an expense is incurred by the firm on behalf of a client and the invoice is addressed to the client, this will not fall to be recorded as part of the firm's VAT records, even if the invoice is settled by the firm and the amount recovered from the client. In that case the invoice must be passed to the client to enable him to account correctly for the VAT. When the invoice is addressed to the firm, however, this must be recorded in the firm's VAT records. Any VAT charged on the invoice will, subject to the normal rules, be treated as VAT input by the firm. When the disbursement is charged out to the client, whether separately disclosed or incorporated in an inclusive fee, VAT must be levied in the normal way.

The firm's expenses

The control and recording of other expenditure by a partnership poses no problems peculiar to that particular form of organisation, and merely requires an appropriate coding system to categorise expenses according to profit or cost centre depending upon the structure of management reporting required (see Chapter 5). The largest single item of expense is normally the payroll and since, apart from overtime payments for some staff, payroll costs are independent of the number of hours actually worked, a conventional payroll system is usually quite adequate, whatever the size of the firm. The only refinement sometimes introduced concerns expenses incurred by staff, which are often repaid to them as part of the salary payment procedure. This cuts down the volume of petty cash that has to be handled by the firm.

The normal principles of control and authorisation of expenditure apply to a partnership. There must be a clear organisational structure and definition of limits of authority. The accounts department must know, for example, who has authority to approve changes in the payroll and expenditure at defined levels. Not all of these matters will necessarily be limited solely to partners. Whether, in a large partnership, some of that authority should be delegated to specific partners or to senior managers is a question already debated in Chapter 1, but if it is, the staff making payments must be aware of the authority of the individuals concerned.

The Balance Sheet

Debtors and creditors

Partnerships usually require few modifications to standard accounting systems for recording debtors and creditors. Debtors, with few exceptions, such as staff loans, will represent unpaid fees and these will require analysis by age and according to the partner raising the fee. In the case of creditors, since professional firms are not buying materials for manufacture, the number of suppliers is often relatively modest and a conventional ledger system may not be needed by the smaller firm. It can perhaps more profitably simply keep a file of unpaid invoices, transferring these to a paid file when settled. Provided a proper control is maintained of these (by using an invoice register and numbering the invoices as they are entered in the register) to ensure that invoices are neither lost nor paid twice, this can often be the most cost effective way of dealing with payments to suppliers, whether on the firm's own account or in respect of disbursements.

Fixed assets

Even if the firm takes the view that it should not, in principle, own fixed assets, it is almost inevitable that it will use, if not own, such items as cars, computers and other office equipment. Whatever policy is adopted for these items in the financial accounts, it is desirable both from the point of view of general control and for insurance purposes that some record be maintained of the principal items. Thus, if even a small fleet of cars is operated, a record of these indicating who uses (and is therefore responsible for) each is obviously essential. Similarly, a record should be kept of valuable but easily moveable items such as micro-computers or sophisticated calculators.

If such items are not written off in the accounts as purchased, such a register should also contain details of the cost, date of purchase and rate of depreciation applied, with the net total shown by the register agreeing with the figures appearing in the firm's annual balance sheet.

Accounting Policies

As well as to provide the information necessary to manage the business during the course of the year, all of the records referred to in the earlier sections of this chapter will be used in the production of the firm's annual accounts. These will represent the definitive statement of the financial result of the business and will quantify the profits which will be shared by partners. It is as well, therefore, for partners to give some thought as to how those profits are to be struck. Having said that, however, it must be remembered that the Inland Revenue have rules on the same subject and it is usually both simpler and more equitable if the firm recognises similar rules in its annual accounts, even though different operational requirements may be incorporated in the management accounts. In that way the profits recognised by the firm will correspond fairly closely to the profits which will form the basis of a tax assessment.

With the foregoing proviso in mind the following principal accounting policies can be considered.

Income

For established partnerships income is normally accounted for on one of three bases:

— cash received;
— fees rendered;
— full earnings.

On the first basis, income is only recognised when cash is received from a client. On the second, income is credited when the fee is

rendered, so that client debtors are included in the firm's accounts.
A firm that adopts the full earnings basis strikes its profit after
carrying forward to the next period the cost applicable to work
done but not billed at the accounting date; in other words it eva-
luates the cost of work in progress at each accounting date. In this
context partners' time is not a cost since partners' remuneration is
an appropriation of profit rather than an expense of the business.

While, in terms of the profits enjoyed year by year, these different bases of accounting may not give markedly different results,
they can over a period result in very different levels of working
capital being required. If, for example, work in progress were to
be introduced into a firm's accounts as an asset (and, for the sake
of simplicity, ignoring the detailed tax rules on the subject), the
consequence would be that greater profits would have been recognised; these would be credited partly to partners and partly to taxation reserves. When the tax liabilities are actually paid this will
give rise to increased working capital requirements and even if
partners do not withdraw the additional amounts credited to them
at the time, they will certainly do so when they retire, thus further
increasing the need for working capital in the firm. It must be
emphasized that this is an over-simplification merely to illustrate
the effect of including work in progress (or debtors) in the
accounts; in particular, in any given year, partners would only be
credited with and pay tax on, any *uplift* in work in progress
between each balance sheet date. Nevertheless, it will be obvious
that a fees rendered basis of accounting will require more working
capital than a cash basis and that a full earnings basis will require
more still. For this reason, firms on either of the first two bases will
normally wish to stay on that basis.

Any of the three methods is acceptable to the Inland Revenue
for a professional partnership but with the important exception
that for new businesses (whether actually new or merely deemed,
for tax purposes, to be new) the Inland Revenue requires the
profits to be computed on the full earnings basis for at least the
first three accounting periods. In addition, those firms on a cash or
fees rendered basis are required to undertake to issue bills on a
regular basis. As there is usually a considerable tax penalty in
changing thereafter to one of the other bases, firms normally then
stay on a full earnings basis. For the reasons mentioned above the
firm's financial accounts should recognise income on whatever
basis has been established with the Inland Revenue. To do otherwise will lead to great difficulty in retaining equity between
partners.

A word of caution, however. Whatever method is adopted it is
essential that all the appropriate costs are included in respect of

whatever income is recognised. If, for example, the profession is one where substantial fees can be rendered at an early stage in an assignment so that a higher proportion of income is recognised than the proportion of costs actually incurred on the assignment up to that point, it is essential that an appropriate accrual of those proportionate costs be included in the accounts. In the case of architects, where contracts might spread over several years, it is inappropriate to recognise as income any fees received until the profit or loss on the total contract can be estimated with reasonable certainty. If fees are treated as income before the results of the contracts can be estimated there is a risk that partners may withdraw and pay tax on sums that are not true profits. This will be inequitable between partners if sharing ratios have changed or partners been admitted or have retired between the two periods. It can also, in extreme cases, lead to cash flow problems if the profits have been withdrawn when they should have been left in the business to finance the subsequent costs.

Expenses

Strictly, if income is accounted for on a cash basis the Inland Revenue may also require expenses to be similarly accounted for, but in practice this is unusual. Thus apart from the direct costs of any jobs fee'd in advance as described above, other expenses should also normally be accounted for on an accruals basis to ensure that a full year's expenses (and no more) are actually charged in arriving at the profits. In particular, if a staff bonus is to be paid by reference to the year's results, this should be accrued before striking the profit attributable to partners.

Fixed assets

If freehold properties are owned by the firm it may be appropriate to provide for the depreciation of the building element as is done by companies. Most firms, however, will hope that their properties are appreciating and they will merely carry them in the balance sheet at cost, or perhaps at a revalued amount if that is provided for by the partnership agreement on the admission or retirement of a partner.

Any premium paid on a leasehold property must clearly be written off over, at most, the remaining life of the lease. The same applies to tenants' fixtures and partitions installed in leasehold properties.

From a strict accounting view point, other assets should be written off over the period during which the firm will enjoy the benefit of the expenditure. The tax rules may, however, not correspond with such a policy. For example, when, for tax purposes, most assets could be written off in full in the year of purchase there was a strong case for following that policy in the firm's own accounts. It resulted in broad consistency between the bearing of the cost and the recognition of the tax relief, even though partners enjoying the benefit of the expenditure might have been different from those bearing the cost. With tax relief now spread over a number of years, substantial items of capital expenditure should also be written off in the firm's accounts over a period, though preferably over a shorter time scale than used by the Inland Revenue, who calculate annual tax allowances on the reducing balance method.

Debtors and disbursements

In every firm there will be some debts that remain outstanding for a significant period. In just the same way as fixed assets should be written off before assessing profits, so should provision be made for old uncollected debts. They have not yet been collected in cash and that cash is therefore not available to partners either to distribute or to finance other working capital requirements.

What constitutes old for this purpose will vary from firm to firm but certainly anything over 12 months old unpaid at the balance sheet date should be provided for and many firms shorten the period to six months. It should be noted, however, that such provisions will only be accepted by the Inland Revenue if there is genuine doubt as to the collectability of specific debts. Disbursements should also be reviewed for the purposes of the annual accounts and any that cannot be recovered from clients must of course be written off.

Form of Financial Accounts

The form of the basic profit and loss account and balance sheet calls for no striking modifications as compared with those for any other business enterprise. An example is set out in Appendices 2.1 and 2.2. The profit and loss account should have expenditure grouped according to whatever suits the needs of the particular business but will commonly encompass the following:

— employee costs (including such ancillary matters as

National Insurance contributions, staff welfare and training
and so on);
— establishments costs (rent, rates, depreciation, repairs,
etc.,);
— office expenses (telephone, stationery, etc.,);
— financial expenses (any interest received or paid, bad debt
provisions and disbursements written off); and
— other costs.

Greater detail of particular account headings (*e.g.* entertaining, or
sundry expenses) can be included in supplementary schedules to
the accounts according to the needs of the partners.

Peculiar to partnerships are of course the capital and drawings
accounts of the partners themselves and the firm's taxation
reserves. An example of how these might be set out in the annual
accounts so as to give each partner a clear statement of his interest
in the firm is given in Appendices 2.3 and 2.4. Appendix 2.3 illustrates only the simple situation where partners maintain merely a
capital account and a drawings account, but the layout can easily
be expanded to incorporate other accounts, *e.g.* the partner's
share of any revaluation in the firm's carrying value of a service
company (see Chapter 11), showing opening and closing balances
and the movement in the period. Some firms prefer not to distribute to partners a schedule showing the profit share of all
partners and if that is the case the detailed schedules can be
retained by the finance partner and a statement prepared for each
partner individually, giving him the requisite information about his
own position. The treatment of tax reserves in the firm's accounts
is considered in Chapter 10.

For some years now, companies and those partnerships whose
accounts are required to give a "true and fair view" have been
required to include a statement of source and application of funds
in their annual accounts but it is comparatively rare to find such a
statement included in a partnership's accounts. Nevertheless,
funds flow is a crucial part of a partnership's business, just as much
as it is of a company's business and it is a useful way of demonstrating to the partners in the firm just what has happened to the firm's
cash and, why if that be the case, the sharply increased level of
working capital required to finance debtors and work in progress
has precluded a full distribution of net profits to partners. In other
words it can be a useful tool for the senior partner or finance
partner in persuading his fellow partners to work harder at sending
out or collecting fees or for the junior partner to persuade his
seniors that the firm is carrying too much cash in the business and
that more of it should be paid out to partners! A suggested format

for a funds statement together with notes on its preparation are given in Appendices 2.6 and 2.7.

Finally, where a firm has custody of clients' money, the annual accounts should show by way of note the amount of clients' money held on clients' account at the bank. As the firm is acting purely as agent of the client in placing the money on client account, the figures should under no circumstances actually be incorporated in the balance sheet as assets and liabilities of the firm.

Formalities

With the exception of partnerships that are members of The Stock Exchange, there is no formal United Kingdom requirement for partnership accounts to be audited. There are, of course, requirements for accountants to report on the custody of clients' money held by solicitors and estate agents. Nevertheless, it is good practice for a firm of accountants to be employed by a partnership to deal not only with such formalities but also to review and report to the partners on the firm's systems of internal control. This will provide a check on the adequacy of the firm's procedures for ensuring that all fees are issued and all debts collected as well as the more obvious features such as control of cash. The accounts of service or other companies owned or associated with partnerships are, of course, required by law to be audited annually.

Once the annual accounts have been finalised and any work on them completed by the firm's accountants, the partners should be asked formally to approve them. Final distribution of the profits, based on those accounts should be dependent on such approval. It is usual for the approval to be evidenced by partners signing the balance sheet.

Understanding the Annual Accounts

While the management and control of the business will require the preparation of regular accounting and other management information as explained in Chapter 5, the distribution of the annual financial accounts gives each partner the opportunity to appraise the financial progress of the business. Each partner therefore needs some appreciation of what conclusions can sensibly be drawn from a reading of the accounts and equally what limitations are inherent in the accounts as a reflection of the business.

The profit and loss account

It is essential that partners are aware which of the three bases has
been used to recognise income in the accounts. Only the full earnings basis will give a reasonable approximation of the results of the
firm's activity during the year. If one of the other bases has been
used and, for example, distributable profits have remained static,
that may conceal the fact that there has been a substantial increase
in unbilled work in progress in the year. On a full earnings basis
that increase would have resulted in a commensurate increase in
disclosed profits. It is helpful, therefore, where a cash or fees rendered basis of accounting is adopted, if the accounts are accompanied by a commentary indicating the effect of any change in the
level of work in progress. The financial accounts should also be
reconciled to the management accounts and any major reconciling
items explained to partners.

Apart from the level of activity, partners will also be interested
in the ratio of expenses to income and thus in the net profit margin
(the ratio of distributable profit to income). For most professional
partnerships by far the largest expense will be staff costs and a
comparison of these as a ratio of fee income (adjusted, if possible,
as explained above, for the increase or decrease in work in progress) is a better guide to whether salaries are under control than a
simple comparison of this year's costs with those of the previous
year. In a small firm, the elevation of a salaried employee to equity
partner can distort such ratios, so allowance might need to be
made for that.

Similar ratios can be calculated for the other main groups of
expenditure as a guide to whether they are moving ahead faster or
slower than income, but care will need to be taken to identify
exceptional items which can distort trends. For instance, one year
may have borne the whole of the costs of a major office refurbish-
ment or a major item of capital expenditure.

The balance sheet

The balance sheet is useful principally as an indication not only of
partners' balances in the firm, but of the firm's working capital
requirements. It must be remembered, however, that the balance
sheet gives the position for only one day, and that might not be a
typical day. Nevertheless, a comparison of work-in-progress and
debtors (when they are included in the accounts) with fees rendered to give the average number of days activity represented by
those assets gives a useful guide as to progress in sending fees out

and collecting the cash more quickly. If, as is often the case, there has been a burst of feeing towards the end of the financial year, that will need to be allowed for in making the calculations. Even where work in progress and debtors are not included in the accounts, it is to be hoped that memorandum records will be available so that such comparisons can still be made.

Commentary

Reference has already been made to the desirability of a commentary on the accounts when these have been drawn up other than on an earnings basis and it will be apparent from the previous paragraphs that information beyond that included in the profit and loss account and balance sheet can often be required if even simple comparisons and ratios are not to be misleading. The annual accounts should therefore always be accompanied by a short commentary prepared by the firm's accountant. If that is prepared by the firm's internal accountant it should nevertheless be made available to the external accountant for comment before being distributed to partners, but more often it will be prepared in the first place by the external accountant. It is also desirable for the external accountant to attend the partners' meeting when the accounts are being considered. This gives him the opportunity of raising any points he thinks should be drawn to the attention of partners and to answer any questions from partners on the accounts.

3 Time Recording

One of the hottest debates in many partnerships is whether there is any need formally to record time, the opponents of such a procedure arguing that it is irrelevant as it makes no difference to what they can charge their clients. But time is a scarce and expensive resource and its control is an integral part of the operational and financial management of many partnerships, particularly, solicitors, accountants and actuaries who traditionally charge for their services by reference to time spent. This chapter deals with some of the features that any time recording system should encompass.

However small the firm, time recording lends itself admirably to computerisation and so long as the business is at least large enough to justify the use of a micro-computer, the time records for even a two partner firm can easily be maintained on a micro-computer in a more effective way than by using hand written records. For larger firms there are many ready made packages on the market suitable for specific professions and these can be used either on the firm's own mini-computer or via a computer bureau. For the largest firms a bespoke system may be justifiable but the expense of this compared with a package system means that for many firms the extra cost is not justified by the benefits obtained.

For the maximum use to be obtained from the information, partners and fee earners should account on their time sheet for at least the standard number of hours in the firm's working week. Naturally some time, especially of senior staff and partners, will be spent on non-chargeable matters, but these should nevertheless be recorded under appropriate headings so that everyone is encouraged to account for the whole of their time. It is then possible to review and more easily control non-chargeable time.

Many firms complete time sheets weekly, but since in most cases fees are not rendered weekly, there is no loss of control over the business and a halving of processing costs if time sheets are completed on a fortnightly basis. Each firm will need to decide what its unit of time measurement will be. This will depend upon the nature of the particular work being performed and on whether a majority of fee earners are dealing with a few or many cases in the course of a day. For most professions a half-hour or quarter-hour unit is appropriate. Some firms use units of five or six minutes and while this gives greater theoretical accuracy it also increases the time required of professional staff to complete a time sheet. As a result it can sometimes lead to greater aggravation amongst staff leading to carelessness in completion and thus defeating the objective of greater accuracy. Another approach is to establish standard units of time for specified functions, *e.g.* writing a letter or making a telephone call but since such activities vary greatly in the time they take this is rarely likely to be a satisfactory method.

The precise way in which the time records are maintained will depend upon the management statistics required from them as discussed in Chapter 5 but from a purely financial point of view any system will require to be able to record hours (or relevant smaller units of time) and evaluate these at rates determined from time to time by the partners. The system should also have the basic facility for eliminating from the time records the particular hours being billed (or written off, if no fee is being rendered) and thus for carrying forward time to be recovered in a subsequent fee. Similarly there should be a facility to accrue for time spent but not yet recorded as, for instance, where a fee is to be rendered ahead of all the relevant work being carried out, or if it has to be sent out urgently. There should also be a facility for ageing the balance of time recorded against any particular client or matter so that this can be reviewed and wherever possible, fees sent in respect of the older matters. This meets the requirement that all work that should give rise to a fee does actually do so. For larger firms it may be appropriate to integrate the time records with the financial records so that when a fee is being entered into the system it updates in one operation both the time records (by eliminating the time billed) and the financial records. If the records are not integrated, fees rendered will have to be processed twice to update both sets of records.

Even where firms do not charge primarily or at all by reference to time, there are compelling reasons for recording time. These include:

— the possibility of achieving better fees (and ensuring that all chargeable work is billed);
— improved management information;
— the need to meet market requirements for demonstrating the time actually spent on an assignment.

Each is considered in turn.

Better feeing

Whatever other factors are taken into account in assessing a fee, a partner should have regard to the time spent on an assignment by him and his staff. The ultimate resource he is selling is time and a measure of time spent is a measure of cost. He will also wish to take into account the level of experience of the staff employed on the job. While not all fees can be influenced by the amount of time spent, it will undoubtedly be useful to the partner in any negotiations over the level of the fee if he is at least aware of the costs of the job as evidenced by the time spent.

The existence of an effective time recording system is of course crucial where time is the principal element taken into account in fixing a fee. In the absence of a record of the time spent, by grade of staff, this information will have to be gathered from other, less precise evidence—from the matter file in the case of a solicitor. This is the familiar role of the solicitor's costs department which may evaluate a matter according to the number of letters, memoranda of interviews and so on. Such a system depends, as does a time recording system, on the efficient recording of data by the fee earner, but it is much less likely that "thinking time" will be evidenced on the matter file than in a formal record of time spent. Further, most professional practitioners are likely to agree that they prefer to charge less rather than more for their services. It is, after all, easier to persuade a client to pay £1,000 than £2,000! It may be less easy to do that if the fee earner is faced with a statement of time spent evaluated at £2,000 and the prospect of explaining to his partners a £1,000 "deficit" on the job. It may at least prompt second thoughts and perhaps enable the fee earner to identify time spent on the job which for one reason or another is not properly reflected in the matter file. It will also encourage the fee earner to think very carefully about the justification for charging less than appears on the time record in the knowledge that this will be reported to his superiors or to his partners. He may therefore seek a higher fee than would otherwise be the case. We have no doubt that in practice, the existence of evaluated time records does indeed enhance the level of feeing achieved. Furthermore, as noted in Chapter 2, its existence is also an important part of the procedure for ensuring that all chargeable work gives rise to a fee.

Improved Management Information

Information about profitability of different types of work, or by type of client, can only be derived from a knowledge of the time spent on each job. There is no other practicable way of assessing the staff costs involved.

Equally important is the ability to assess the level and value of work in progress, even where, for firms that account for profits on a cash received or fees rendered basis there is no need for this value to be included in the firm's accounts. Without knowing the extent of any change in the value of work in progress between the beginning and end of a period it is impossible to know whether an increase in fees rendered in that period represents an improvement in the level of work carried out or is simply the result of a change in the level of work in progress. Such knowledge is crucial to a judgement of the true profitability of the firm.

A time recording system that accounts for a full 35 or 40 hours each week also enables information to be produced on the amount of time spent on non-feeable activities, be they the administration of the firm, or time spent developing a new product or service. The latter is particularly important. A properly managed firm will have decided to spend time on such a development on the basis of assumptions as to the likely time required coupled with the potential return. It is crucial therefore to monitor the time actually spent against time budgeted to be spent and also to ensure that the total cost of the investment is recorded so that a judgement can ultimately be made on the adequacy of the return on that investment.

As suggested above a report of deficits (or surpluses) on fees compared with time spent evaluated at standard rates is also a useful tool. Clearly the information must be handled sensitively if partners and staff are not to feel threatened, but most professional people are influenced by peer pressure and do not like to be out of step.

Market Requirements

All professions are now faced with a more competitive environment where their costs and fees are subject to close scrutiny. For government work, in particular, individual fee rates are usually required to be negotiated for each grade of staff to be employed on a job and the ultimate justification of the fee rendered may require the production of evidence of time actually incurred in the form of a statement of time spent produced by the firm's own time recording system. Without that facility firms are obviously at a disadvantage in such a business environment.

For all the above reasons, therefore, professional firms, which by definition are selling time, should consider carefully the potential benefits to be derived from maintaining a time recording system even if they do not calculate their fees by direct reference to time actually spent.

4 Planning and Budgeting

Chapter 2 dealt with the recording of firms' actual financial performance leading to the production of financial accounts and as a means of enabling the enterprise to deal with third parties—to pay its creditors and to collect its debts; in other words how firms should record what actually happened.

But if a firm is to be successful as a business it needs to take a view on what it wants to do in the future, how this will be affected by the business environment in which it operates and how its actual performance compares with what it hoped to do. It must plan ahead. Planning can be categorised at two levels—the longer term planning of strategic decisions, *e.g.* moving to larger premises or developing a completely new business activity, and short term budgeting up to say 12 months ahead. But no plans, long or short term, can be expected to be achieved in their entirety and in every detail. For the best use to be obtained from them comparison of actual performance against at least the short term plan (the budget) is a necessary pre-requisite to taking management action so that the firm is better able to achieve its plans. This chapter therefore considers long term planning and budgeting; the following chapter deals with the reporting of the actual results.

Long Term Planning

Many partners express the view that it is impossible to know what is going to happen next week, still less to look 12 months ahead, and that to try to plan even further ahead is a complete waste of time. Usually such views are based upon the premise that what is being attempted is a prediction of a future financial result. While that may be true of a short term profit or cash forecast it is not necessarily true of a 12 month budget and is certainly not the purpose of long range planning. The purpose of looking ahead for such a period is to enable a business to take the strategic decisions that are likely to be most appropriate to the future needs of the enterprise. To take an obvious example, a firm may have experienced a period of rapid growth such that it needs more office space. Without perhaps consciously formulating a business plan, most partners will make some kind of subjective judgement of how much more growth they expect over the next few years and how much space they believe the firm is likely both to require and to be able to afford, before deciding on the size and location of new premises. All that a business plan seeks to do is to enable partners to consider all the major factors likely to affect their business, to make an assessment of the interaction of those factors upon one another, and therefore to be better prepared to cope with the development of the business.

The principal factors likely to be considered by most firms when looking ahead are:

— the size of the firm's existing market and partners' assessment of possible future changes in that market;
— the present competitive pressures in the firm's markets and whether these are thought likely to change;
— the possibility that existing markets will decline or disappear altogether or that new ones will appear;
— the likely availability of suitable personnel at all grades, including an adequate flow of potential new partners;
— the scale of financial resources likely to be available to the firm from both internally generated and external sources;
— the partners' own aspirations as to the size and type of firm they wish to be part of and the level of financial reward that they hope to achieve from the business;
— the growth of technology and its impact on the firm;
— the effect of changes in outside factors, *e.g.* new legislation or economic change on the firm and its clients.

The answers to a number of those questions are capable of expression in financial terms and it may be necessary to produce alternative figures as part of the process of coming to an agreed answer to the questions. Having done so, it is then possible to express the plan in terms of an outline financial statement, showing income, expenses (even if only as single figures for each of personnel, property and other costs), capital employed and sources of capital. From that outline financial model can then be developed more specific objectives which are seen to be appropriate to the achievement of the desired result. These might be expressed as increasing the firm's income from a particular market sector by or to a given percentage of the firm's total income over a defined period, or achieving an increased geographical coverage by establishing new offices in a defined region over a given number of years.

Expressed in terms such as these, most partners find less difficulty in perceiving both the need for and the use of planning, for such plans are self-evidently not a prediction of what is going to happen. They are a statement of objectives supported by outline strategies designed to achieve those objectives. The preparation of a plan on these lines will probably suggest how far ahead it is practicable for the individual firm to look. To be of maximum use in managing the firm it should certainly cover a two or three year period but it is unlikely that, at this level of detail, anything more than a five year period will prove useful.

It must be stressed that one of the main benefits of such planning is the active discussion by partners of potential future opportunities and problems. Their consideration will lead to creative thinking and planning and will help to avoid the pitfalls of "management by surprise." The nature of the plan will give some guidance as to when and how often it should be reviewed. If it covers only two years forward then clearly it must be reviewed and rolled forward for a further year at the end of year one. There may be less need, however, to roll forward a five year plan on an annual basis. Certainly, it should be reviewed annually, but it may be unnecessary to produce a completely new plan more frequently than every two or three years. Much will also depend, of course, upon how the business actually fares compared with its plan. If everything is on course, there is unlikely to be much required by way of review or up-dating the plan. But if not, it may be that the plan itself is seen to be no longer appropriate and the partners will need to redefine their objectives and prepare a new plan. Discussions of such plans are best held away from the pressures and interruptions of the daily office routine. There is much to be said for the partners meeting for a day or half a day away from the office at least once a year to discuss the firm's objectives and plans. If such a meeting is well planned, with an agenda and discussion papers, it can achieve a great deal in helping partners clarify their thinking and thus in helping the development of the business strategy. By contrast an ill-planned meeting of this type can prove extremely counter-productive.

Budgeting

The purpose of budgeting

In contrast to the long term plan the budget should cover only a single financial year and it should be prepared and agreed before the start of the year. Since it covers a much shorter period than the long term plan, greater detail and accuracy is both possible and appropriate, but as with the plan, the purpose is not to make a prediction of eventual detailed financial performance of the firm. It is designed to show what the financial result will be if the firm performs in accordance with a set of agreed business assumptions. It can then be compared periodically with actual performance, thus enabling management to take decisions, where it considers it appropriate, designed to correct any undesirable deviations from the budget.

The process of budgeting itself can also lead to management action. For example, if the initial assumptions made as to fee income and expenses show that an unacceptably low profit will be generated, it is open to management to take corrective action at that stage. That might be to reduce staff numbers or to increase charging rates if either of those steps was thought practicable or if not it might lead to a more fundamental reappraisal; does the firm need more or fewer partners, or should it seek an acquisition or merger?

It should be apparent from the foregoing that once a budget has been prepared and agreed there is usually no purpose in refining or amending it as the year progresses. This is only likely to be worthwhile if circumstances have changed so dramatically that the shape of the business has had to be materially changed. In those circumstances the original figures cease to be useful as a standard against which to compare actual results and a new budget would be appropriate. But there is no point in spending time adjusting the budget for the normal variations in staff numbers or salary rates not incorporated in the original budget. That is not to say that part way through the year a forecast of the eventual profit should not be made. Particularly towards the end of the year a detailed projection of the likely outcome can often be useful in order to ensure that the requisite value of fees is indeed achieved. But there is little point in taking the trouble to replace the budget by such a forecast. The improvement in management decisions that might be achieved thereby is not likely to justify the time and expense incurred.

Preparing the budget

The first stage in the budgeting process is the preparation of the business plan for the year. This will be more detailed than the long term plan but must be consistent with it. It should be prepared by the executive committee/managing partner and will provide the framework for the budget. It will need to take account of new business areas and will require assumptions on such matters as growth rates, fee rates, salary levels and any special features applicable in the year, perhaps the development of a new project or a move to new premises. The preparation of the budget can then proceed.

Who should prepare the budget? "The partnership accountant" say the partners with one voice. To put the primary responsibility for the creation of the budget on the accountant is a very great mistake. The object of the budget is to help the firm achieve its plan; more specifically to help it achieve the desired level of income and expenditure. Those preparing the budget must therefore be those who will be in a position to take responsibility for the firm's performance. It is partners and fee-earners alone who are in a position to influence fee income and it is they, therefore, who must be involved in the preparation of the fee budget and accept the final figures. The accountant will, of course, be able to assist in converting the assumptions made by the partners into hard figures and in collating the figures. He will also, probably, be the most appropriate person to prepare the overhead budget as it is he who will be in a position to exercise some management control over that expenditure. But if he is asked to produce the fee budget (or indeed the salary budget for fee-earning staff) he will have to make judgements about other people's responsibilities and those other people will tend to dismiss the budget as irrelevant as they were not involved in its preparation. The ideal approach is a joint exercise between the fee earners (or those partners responsible for them) and the finance partner and partnership accountant.

The final form of an annual budget should be a profit and loss account, balance sheet and cash projection. Supporting this will be the detailed budgets for each profit centre and cost centre, with separate projections for personnel budgets including budgets of chargeable hours; these are a necessary step in formulating a salaries budget and an income budget respectively. Capital expenditure must also be budgeted. The main headings can be considered in turn.

Income budget

This is often the most difficult figure to develop satisfactorily for a budget. While, as we have said, the main purpose of the budget is not to be a forecast, it is clearly important that the assumptions used in its preparation are as realistic as possible. So far as income is concerned this can be approached in two different ways—an assessment of the fee or commission income that the firm's known or prospective clients are thought likely to produce, and an assessment of the fee earning capacity of the partners and professional staff. Both methods should be employed and if they give substantially different results that may indicate an imbalance between the number of staff and the anticipated level of business. The estimate of the fee income to be produced by clients is the more difficult of the two. For professions such as accountants or actuaries with an element of recurring work from the same clients there is obviously a base from which to develop a fee budget, but for, say, lawyers or surveyors with minimal recurring work a different technique is required. The precise mechanics will have to be developed by each firm to suit its needs, but it is usually helpful if trends from prior periods are examined and if statistical information on past performance is maintained. Thus a firm of solicitors may find it helpful to analyse its fees by type of service offered and to examine the trend of numbers of matters fee'd by month or quarter, the average value of each fee and the average fee rate achieved in respect of each hour spent on the matter. Each of these may reveal trends which, taken in conjunction with the partners' view of the business climate generally and specific knowledge of the likely level of activity of at least some of their clients, can be extrapolated forward to give an initial view of fee income. Similarly, an estate agent can make use of statistics on the number of new properties in different categories coming onto his register each month and the average length of time properties are on the register before a sale is achieved. Likewise, consultants can assess the trend of enquiries received and the proportion of enquiries that are converted into fee paying assignments in each category of business. If such a process has not been attempted before, the results may well not be too accurate to start with, but over a period most firms find that it is possible to predict, within acceptable limits, at least a base level of income.

The alternative approach of estimating the fee-earning capacity of partners and staff is normally easier. For those firms that maintain time records and traditionally charge by reference to time spent, the matter becomes a simple calculation for each person of the number of chargeable hours expected in the year (on the basis of past performance) times the charging rate for that particular grade of person. The sum of those calculations for all fee-earners then represents, in effect, the productive capacity of the firm which can be measured against the fee income as previously calculated. The figures may require adjustment if the firm regularly earns surpluses or incurs deficits compared with the standard charging rates. Where the firm does not maintain time records and/or it does not charge by reference to time spent such calculations are not possible, but similar principles can be employed in as much as a judgement can be made, by reference to past performance, of the number and value of fees that particular staff or grades of staff can be expected to produce. This again is, in effect, an assessment of the firm's productive capacity. If in either case, the productive capacity appears to be below the expected level of fee income, that might be an indication that more staff are required or it might simply mean that the original fee estimate was too optimistic. Conversely, an excess of productive capacity over expected fee income might be an indication that the firm is carrying too many staff or it is pricing them at too high a rate for the market.

Both methods of preparing an income budget require assumptions as to sales prices, be they expressed as rates per hour or as a percentage of the value of the work executed or sales value achieved for the client. How should sales pricing be decided? It is worth remembering, at the outset, the two principal factors that operate in the determination of prices: what the market will bear, and the costs, including allowance for a reasonable profit, of the provider of the goods or ssservice.

Costs can be assessed in greater or lesser detail, according to needs, by reference to the firm's systems of management information described in the next chapter. In arriving at costs, whether by type of work or by grade of employee, some judgement will need to be made of the proportion of the fee-earning time that will be sent on non-feeable work. The cost per hour or per assignment for an employee who spends 1,000 hours per annum on chargeable matters is obviously greater than for another of the same grade who achieves 1,500 chargeable hours in the year. Such information can obviously only be obtained if the firm operates a comprehensive system of time recording.

But while it is important to know one's costs, there are few, if any, firms that can charge on the basis of cost-plus. A knowledge of what the market will bear and what one's competitors are charging is therefore crucial. The most obvious and accurate knowledge for an established firm is its experience over the past year. Partners will be able to assess how price sensitive their clients have been and therefore make a judgement as to whether they will be able to increase prices at a greater or lesser rate than the expected level of inflation. A helpful, but not necessarily wholly accurate, means of assessing the market is to exchange price information with one's competitors. It may not be accurate because, wittingly or not, the information may not have been produced on precisely the same basis *e.g.* one firm's hourly rates may be designed to recover all indirect costs including typists' salaries, whereas another firm may charge separately for typists' time. Also, for firms charging by reference to time, the amount of time spent on an assignment is obviously just as important as the rate per hour and that can be a difficult matter to compare. For commission based professions, however, a simple comparison of percentages is probably easily made and quite reliable, especially for those offering a retail service such as residential house agency where a telephone enquiry will usually elicite the level of any discount being offered below the standard rates.

The new firm, with no track record, will have to rely on whatever market information it can obtain. If a comparison of the rates thus suggested with its projected costs give either an unusually favourable result or look particularly unsatisfactory, that might mean that either prices or costs have been poorly assessed and that more careful analysis is required.

For all types of firm, participation in inter-firm comparisons may be helpful in assessing financial performance, but especially in the case of the large schemes, there may be difficulty in ensuring that the figures are truly comparable. A more useful result can often be obtained if a group of comparable firms get together and exchange information on a confidential basis through an intermediary such as an accountant. The intermediary can then ensure that the comparisons being made are those most relevant to the group in question and that the figures are truly comparable.

The final point to stress in connection with an income budget is that whatever method of accounting for income is used in the firm's annual accounts, the budget must be prepared on a full earnings (as distinct from a fees rendered or cash received) basis as this is the only realistic measure of profit for control and comparison purposes. A separate adjustment can then be made if the annual accounts are drawn up on a different basis.

Salaries budget

Once agreement has been reached on the income budget and that has been reconciled to the productive capacity of the fee earners it is a simple matter to produce a personnel budget. This will simply be a budget by profit or cost centre of the numbers of staff required at each grade allowing for expected recruitment, promotions and retirements. Any unexpected resignations should not affect the personnel budget as they will presumably be replaced. The only impact will be the additional recruitment costs for which there should be a separate budget. Given an agreed personnel budget, that can then be converted into a salaries budget by applying known salary rates and allowing for whatever has been agreed by management as the appropriate rate of increase for the salary reviews due during the year.

Overheads budget

Producing the overheads budget is normally a matter of common sense. The majority of overheads in a professional practice are fixed in the sense that they do not vary directly in relation to the level of fee income. Accordingly, it is usually appropriate to take the current level of expenditure at the time of the preparation of the budget and to adjust this for known or expected increases or decreases and any special factors that will apply in the year. These will include inflationary increases (in which case an assumption will have to be made as to the level at which inflation is expected to run over the budget period) or increases arising from changes in the operations of the firm, *e.g.* more or less space occupied and therefore changes in the rent and rates charge, or higher depreciation because of investment in new word processors. Interest receivable or payable will be derived from the cash forecast (see below) the projected interest rate being applied to the forecast monthly cash balance or overdraft.

Budgeted profit

Having budgeted income, salaries and overheads all the constituent parts of the profit and loss account have been dealt with. All that remains is to summarise these by profit and cost centre and calculate the budgeted profit. As indicated above, management action may be required at that point if the budgeted results are unsatisfactory either for a particular profit or cost centre or for the firm as a whole, but if the figures are agreed, the next step is to prepare a cash flow forecast.

Cash forecasts

As with plans and budgets, the purpose of cash forecasts needs to be understood. They are not intended, except in the very short term, to be a prediction of the bank balance or overdraft at any given date. They are intended to show the likely level of cash generation or overdraft required on the assumption that the firm meets its profit budget and on the assumptions as to levels of debtors and creditors, capital expenditure, partners' drawings and so on. The purpose of forecasting cash generation or the likely maximum overdraft level is to enable the firm to plan its finances so that any capital expenditure is allowed for, adequate working capital is available to fund any expected increase in work in progress and debtors and so that partners can plan on a reasonably assured level of monthly drawings. It will also enable the firm to arrange well ahead any additional finance which is shown to be required.

The foregoing comments apply to the 12 month cash forecast that is derived from and is consistent with the profit budget. In addition, for the very reason that it is not possible to predict accurately, for up to a year ahead, the precise timing of receipts from fees, a short term cash forecast for three months ahead should be prepared and updated each month on a rolling three months basis. The purpose of such a short term forecast is indeed to predict, as accurately as possible, the bank balance, or overdraft so that fine tuning of the timing of payments can, where possible and appropriate, be planned, and any necessary fee chasing undertaken.

Preparing the cash forecast

The starting points for the 12 month cash forecast are the profit budget and the expected opening balance sheet for the period of the forecast. From that balance sheet will be drawn the figures for the opening levels of debtors, disbursements and creditors which will be needed for the calculation of the opening month's receipts and payments. The fee budget must then be broken down by month of feeing and spread according to the expected month of receipt of the cash. In the same way, budgeted salaries and expenses must be analysed according to when the payments are expected to be made. Other aspects, not directly incorporated in the profit budget will also need to be allowed for. These will include VAT, payments of income tax and partners' drawings and capital expenditure while items in the budget that do not involve the movement of cash (normally only depreciation) must be excluded from the cash flow. A format for the presentation of a cash forecast and notes on the calculation of some of the items form Appendices 3.1 and 3.2.

The principles to be followed in the preparation of the short term forecast are no different, but a greater degree of accuracy, especially of receipts from fees rendered, should be possible since, at least for the first month of the forecast the expected cash receipts can be related to fees that have already been issued. Care must be taken when reviewing both short and long term forecasts to make due allowance for peaks and troughs in cash demands within each monthly period. The incidence of the normal payment dates for major items such as salaries and VAT, together with past experience, will give a guide as to the likely margin required to cover such fluctuations.

Forecast balance sheet

The final step in the forecasting process is the preparation of a forecast balance sheet at the end of the forecast period. This will be derived from the opening balance sheet, the profit budget and the cash flow forecast. The purpose of preparing a forecast balance sheet is not so much as a direct aid to management but as a means of checking not only the reasonableness of the budget and cash forecast but also on the arithmetical completeness and accuracy of the budgeting exercise. An example of a forecast balance sheet is shown in Appendix 3.5 and the mechanics of its preparation are illustrated in Appendices 3.6, 3.7. It will be seen that it is not much more than an arithmetical exercise. But if the forecast balance sheet reveals figures for debtors or creditors or tax reserves or indeed any balance sheet caption that look unreasonable by comparison with the opening balance sheet or by reference to what might intuitively have been expected, this may on investigation reveal an error in the preparation of the forecasts. For example, it might be the result of an error of calculation (say in the period of debtors collection) or of an assumption which clearly, by reference to the figures produced, is unrealistic (perhaps an inappropriate period of credit from suppliers as revealed by creditors increasing dramatically even though the business has not expanded to the same extent). Any such apparent anomalies must be investigated and, if necessary, corrected before the budget and cash forecasts are finalised and approved by the partners.

5 Reporting the Results

The previous chapter explained that one of the main purposes of budgeting is to provide a yardstick against which to measure actual performance. Once a budget has been prepared variations from budget can then be reviewed to see whether any corrective action is necessary or possible to ensure the continued prosperity of the business. If that purpose is to be achieved, the actual results must be produced promptly and with a reasonable degree of accuracy. It is better to have approximately correct figures available a week or two after the period end than to wait three months for figures which may be a little more accurate but which would lead to no better decisions being taken.

Actual results can be compared with prior year figures, but care must be taken in drawing conclusions. A 10 per cent. increase in fee income over last year may be encouraging, but if the budget increase is 20 per cent. (to recover much higher salary costs in the current year) a comparison with last year will be misleading if not dangerous.

Reporting Structure

The preparation of the budget and the reporting of the results must reflect the structure used by the firm for managing its business. Information must be presented so that those taking management decisions are informed about those areas for which they have direct responsibility. Such an organisational structure often develops in a haphazard manner, and if a management reporting structure is being implemented for the first time or being reviewed, it is essential that the way in which the firm is organised and managed is reappraised before decisions are made on reporting.

Typically, even in a small firm, there will be a degree of departmentalisation based upon such factors as different areas of professional expertise, different types of client or different offices of the practice. In larger firms, a single department offering a uniform range of professional services may itself be divided, simply to produce a group small enough to be managed effectively.

Each of these types of divisions can be used as a basis for management. As a minimum, they will probably be used as a means of allocating staff resources, but in many instances they will form a natural unit for the control of fee income, direct professional costs and some overheads. Thus, in an accountant's practice, it is common to find the firm divided into audit, tax and consultancy departments. A surveyor's business might similarly be divided into investment, valuation, building and other departments. In multi-office firms it would be natural for each office to represent a primary management unit. Each firm must therefore identify its existing management structure and then design its reporting procedures accordingly.

In addition to such functional reporting, however, most firms will wish to have information about the extent and profitability of work of different types and for different sorts of client. Such analyses may cut across the reporting required for direct management control. For example, a firm of architects may have a reputation in particular fields, say hospitals or office refurbishments, in which all of its operational departments participate. It will then be necessary to have two forms of reporting—one for the departments and another for the type of work.

In many firms it is usual to find a degree of resistance to departmental reporting in case this reveals that one type of service is inherently less profitable than another. For example, a solicitor may maintain a residential conveyancing department primarily as a service to executives of its corporate clients and as such be prepared to see a lower level of profitability in that department. Partners responsible for that service must not be criticised for that lower level of profitability. They should be judged by reference to their previously agreed budget and not by reference to the profitability of other departments. But it is only sensible that all partners should be aware of the different levels of profitability expected of each department. Failure to meet those expectations would indeed require review and, if necessary, management action.

Level of Reporting

Once the firm's management structure has been determined, the reporting structure can be designed. This should be in the form of a pyramid, with the greatest detail going to individual partners and managers and progressively summarised information going to each level of management. An overview of a reporting structure is given in Appendix 4.1. It will be obvious from what has so far been written that it is not possible to devise a standard reporting package—

there is no standard firm. But the appropriate features of the over-view, discussed in the following paragraphs, can be developed by each firm to suit its own requirements. In particular, while the overview and the formats set out in Appendix 4 will need to be developed in some detail for the large multi-department firm, a small single office practice may require no more than two simple profit centre reports (showing the profit contribution by each of two departments) a summary of unallocated overheads and some basic statistics (for instance the number of new cases taken on, the average value of each fee rendered or, if time records are main-tained, information about the percentage of time spent on charge-able matters).

Profit Centres

The cornerstone of any reporting system is the profit centre. It is therefore convenient to start with this, even though it is in the middle of the reporting pyramid. The profit centre is that division, department or office within the business responsible for control-ling a section of the firm's income and direct costs. The partner or partners responsible for each profit centre will have budgeted for, and need to know the actual level of, fees, direct staff costs and direct overheads. A summarised form for reporting the results of a profit centre is given in Appendix 4.2. That form envisages report-ing profits after allocating to each profit centre a proportion of all the firm's indirect costs. That is essential for the firm's overall management as it recognises the fact that no individual depart-ment can operate without, *e.g.* an accounts department and that a true measure of profitability must take this into account. The cal-culation of appropriate charging rates is also facilitated, since they must recover not only departmental costs but also the central costs, and still leave an adequate profit margin.

Nevertheless, there is an argument for not allocating costs to departments if those running the department cannot, in that capacity, control the level of those costs. For this reason some firms prefer to report the results of profit centres only down to the contribution level; that is the contribution made by the depart-ment to central costs and overheads after charging professional staff salaries and all directly controllable overheads, such as the costs of secretarial support staff within the department, and accommodation costs.

For this purpose, professional staff costs should include a notional salary for partners, otherwise misleading results will be obtained, particularly when a senior manager becomes a partner.

If no notional salary is charged, the profitability or contribution of a profit centre will appear to have been improved simply as a result of that change of status. Comparisons between profit centres may also be misleading without such a notional charge.

Where analysis of results is required by type of business and this equates with a profit centre—*e.g.* a solicitor's litigation department—the profit centre reporting obviously serves both purposes. But where the same type of work is carried out by several profit centres, a separate analysis will be required. In this instance it may be appropriate to report the results down to the level of fee income less professional staff costs. It is unlikely to be necessary or appropriate to take them to the level of full recovery of all central overheads.

As well as reporting the level of fees against budget, it will also be appropriate, where time records are maintained, to compare the value, at standard charging rates, of the time spent on work for which fees have been rendered with the actual amount of those fees, thus showing an aggregate surplus or deficit. There should also be produced a detailed list of any such deficits exceeding either a given money amount or a given percentage of the fee. The reasons for these deficits can then be examined and any necessary management action taken. That might be a decision to avoid such assignments in future or to encourage fee earners to charge more for that type or work.

On the assumption that time records are maintained, a summary of the amount of time spent in the period in question on chargeable work valued at standard rates should be prepared for each profit centre. Subject to any eventual surpluses or deficits compared with standard rates, this will represent a measure of the amount of saleable work done within the profit centre in the period. As such it is a critical piece of information, requiring immediate investigation if there is any significant shortfall, compared with budget, in either hours or value.

Full time recording will also enable an analysis to be made between chargeable and non-chargeable time. This is a measure of productivity and is also important when assessing costs per employee (see Chapter 4). Non-chargeable time can usefully be analysed between office administration, practice development, training, holidays, sickness and (in the event that it should arise) unoccupied time.

Whether or not time recording is used, some measure of the level of work in progress is essential if the firm's investment in un-billed work is to be controlled. When time recording is used, work in progress can be measured in both hours and value (at standard charging rates) and the number of weeks' input it represents can be calculated. Where there are inadequate time records some assessment must be made by reference to the number of cases or assignments in hand but un-billed.

The firm's investment in debtors must also be monitored and for this purpose the amounts due to the firm in respect of each profit centre's activities should be analysed between current debts and those over, say, three months old. Any action required to reduce the amount of old debtors can then be focussed on the relevant profit centre and, through that, to the individual partners whose clients need to be chased for payment.

In most professional firms, staff costs are the largest single expense and, in the short term, relatively fixed. Effective control can therefore be achieved by reporting simply numbers of staff by broad category.

Cost Centres

As the name suggests cost centres are used for categorising expenses; they do not themselves generate income. They will commonly be the accounts, administration and personnel departments. In larger firms these main areas may be sub-divided for such functions as research, library, training and recruitment. It may also be appropriate to treat finance costs as a separate cost centre. A form of reporting for a cost centre is given in Appendix 4.3.

Allocation of Overheads

Overheads such as accommodation costs, which are under the control of those responsible for profit centres may need to be allocated between profit centres. If central costs incurred by the cost centres are also to be allocated to profit centres, some method for achieving these allocations must be devised. Common methods used are:

— *pro rata* to the number of people employed in each profit/
  cost centre;
— *pro rata* to the relevant salary costs;
— according to the space occupied;
— in the case of use of computers/word processors, etc.,
  according to the measured time used or capacity absorbed.

Common sense will dictate which method is appropriate to any particular type of expense. Allocation by reference to fee income, while sometimes used, is not satisfactory as the level of fee income usually bears little direct relationship to the level of overhead costs. It is important that all departments agree on the basis of allocation at the budgeting stage in order to avoid subsequent arguments about the appropriateness of the costs charged to departments.

Individual Partners

Each partner will require information about his performance in relation to his own clients. This is likely to include fees rendered, surpluses or deficits in relation to expected charging or cost rates for the staff used, levels and age of work in progress and outstanding debtors. The information on these subjects will largely mirror that reported at profit centre level, but on an individual partner and job by job basis.

Projects

When a firm embarks on a new project, *e.g.* the development of a new computerised service which it considers it will be able to sell to clients, it is important that the likely development costs are both budgeted before approval is given to the project and monitored during its progress. Those costs will include staff and partner time (and any related overheads) as well as direct costs paid to third parties. It will also be important to monitor and report revenue in due course. The eventual return on the investment will be of interest to partners both in its own right and when they come to consider the next project put forward for development. A form of project reporting is illustrated in Appendix 4.4.

Other Information

The information that can be produced about a business is legion. Much of it can best be utilised if converted into ratios or percentages and for each business a selection of key statistics can be developed. These can then be reported for the whole firm and, as appropriate, by profit centre and by individual partner and fee earner. A selection of commonly used statistics is listed in Appendix 4.5.

The Firm as a Whole

The apex of the reporting pyramid is the summarised information presented to the management committee and/or the managing/ senior partner. Assuming full allocation of overheads to profit centres, this will represent the summation of the profit centres' results for the period. If overheads are not fully allocated, they will be shown as a direct charge from the cost centres after summarising the profit centre contributions.

In addition to the monthly summaries based on the profit centre results, full quarterly accounts should be prepared including a balance sheet. The final quarter's accounts each year will form the basis for the annual accounts. There will, however, probably be differences between the management and financial accounts beyond matters of presentation and simple fine tuning. If, for financial and tax purposes, the firm accounts on a cash or fees rendered basis, an adjustment to reflect the value of work done not fee'd (plus not received in cash, if appropriate) will be required. Since the management accounts must be prepared on a work done basis—that is the only reliable measure of the profitability of the firm—it is important that the firm is managed by reference to that measure, even if partners and the Inland Revenue share in the results calculated on a different basis. Firms will commonly write-off in the financial accounts the costs of new projects or new equipment as incurred, whereas for management control purposes it is desirable to write these off in the future periods which benefit from the expenditure. An adjustment will therefore be required for this purpose when preparing the financial accounts.

Cash Control

While the single most important element of cash control is the management by individual partners and fee-earners of work in progress and debtors, the cash management of the firm can only be effectively controlled centrally. This is the purpose of the three months' rolling cash forecast. The degree of accuracy required in the preparation of this forecast will depend on the extent of the cash resources available to the firm compared with its perceived needs, but even if there appears to be a substantial margin available to cover contingencies, the forecast should always be prepared to ensure that a major item (perhaps payment for a significant piece of capital expenditure) is not overlooked. Indeed, if there appears to be a permanently available surplus margin, consideration should be given to accelerating partners' drawings.

Review

No firm is static and no reporting system is therefore ever wholly appropriate. It is essential that reports are regularly reviewed for their usefulness and developed, modified or abandoned as appropriate. Discussion with the users is essential in this process. Only in this way will it be discovered what information is actually found to be useful to those managing the business. It may be that greater summarisation or more detail is needed or that tables of figures can perhaps more helpfully be presented as graphs or trend lines. It is an important function of the managing and finance partner to ensure that partners and managers have the best information available to them in a form which they can digest easily, can understand and can act upon.

6 Capital

The Firm's Needs

There are normally two things about the firm's affairs that attract the immediate attention of partners—the amount and division of profits and the requirement for each of them to put up capital. The two are closely linked, but before either can be examined it is necessary to look at the capital requirements of the firm as a whole. That forms the subject of this chapter, which also examines the means by which capital requirements can be kept under control, the alternative sources of capital and the basis upon which capital should be contributed by individual partners.

The Use of Capital

The major requirement for capital in professional partnerships is normally to finance debtors and work-in-progress. The fact that work-in-progress or debtors may not appear in the firm's annual accounts does not mean that they do not exist and thus do not have to be financed. In those circumstances the finance will take the form partly of delayed recognition and hence drawing of profits; thus the funding is also "off balance sheet." It is no less real than the undrawn profits which appear in the balance sheet. Whatever the nature of the profession being conducted it will be necessary to pay for staff salaries and the cost of office premises and other overheads before the work represented by those salaries can be converted into fee or commission income. There will then normally be a further delay before the bill is paid by the client and thus converted into cash in the firm's hands. Many firms are also required to expend cash on disbursements on behalf of clients before they are able to collect the cash from the clients. All of these outlays have to be financed.

Most partnerships will also be obliged to spend money on fixed assets. At the very least office furniture and equipment will be required but increasingly large sums are likely to have to be found for computers and other electronic gadgetry, leasehold premises (where fitting out costs can be very substantial) and cars for both partners and staff. Each of those types of fixed asset is a wasting asset. Some firms invest in genuine fixed assets in the form of a freehold of the premises occupied by the firm. Whilst, as an investment proposition, that might be a good decision it is almost certainly a bad decision as far as the professional partnership is concerned. The capital outlay will place a heavy burden on partners, over and above that with which they are already faced in providing of working capital and will add to the problems of partner succession. Not only will it become difficult for new partners to find their shares of the required capital, but, in extreme cases, the retiring partner might be forced to look outside the firm for an individual or company prepared to inject replacement equity capital. These circumstances are likely to lead to stresses between partners and to divert them from the main business of practising their profession.

The Level of Capital

It is not possible to determine an appropriate level of fixed capital by reference to any formula or ratio. Some firms seek to relate capital to a proportion or multiple of annual expenditure but the application of an arbitrary formula does not, of itself, ensure that the resulting figure is appropriate. Instead, the likely requirements of the firm need to be projected in the form of the regular annual cash forecasts described in Chapter 4. Those cash forecasts should allow not only for all the routine income and expenditure but also partners' drawings, including the withdrawal, to an agreed time-scale as explained below, of the whole of the balance of the previous year's profits after proper provision for taxation. That exercise will demonstrate one of three possibilities:

— there is adequate cash available to meet the firm's needs
— there is surplus cash
— there is inadequate cash.

The first possibility is obviously satisfactory, though it may conceal a slackness in feeing and debt collection procedures which, if tightened up, could create surplus cash resources. The second possibility may also be acceptable, but if the surplus is substantial and can reasonably be seen as continuing, there is no reason why it should not be paid out to partners, subject to leaving an appropriate margin for contingencies. That will have the effect of reducing the partners' funds invested in the business. The third possibility is clearly not satisfactory and if the shortfall cannot be reduced by tighter control of working capital or covered by borrowings, the partners will be forced to put up more capital themselves. That might be by an immediate cash introduction if the matter is urgent, but if the firm has planned its affairs properly the need will have been foreseen in good time and it may be met by withholding part of the profit distribution. The effect in either of these circumstances is that partners's capital will have been increased. By either distributing surplus cash or increasing partners' capital contribution we get to a situation where the capital required of partners is set at a minimum. Leaving aside undrawn profits of the current year and any residue of profits from the previous year, payment of which has been planned and allowed for in the cash flow, any other balances left in by partners will, by definition, represent the fixed capital of the firm. Those balances should be recognised as such and appropriately categorised in the firm's accounts so that there is no expectation that those sums will be payable to partners other than on retirement or withdrawal from the firm.

The Effect of Inflation

Most firms will hope to grow in real terms and should thus expect the requirement for capital to grow as well. But consider the position of a firm with no real growth and inflation running at 5 per cent. per annum. Figures on a per partner basis might be as follows:

		£
Income		108,000
Salaries	36,000	
Overheads	39,000	75,000
Profit (30%)		33,000
Tax at say 40% average rate		13,200
Net profit per partner		£19,800

If debtors equate to three months' bills plus VAT, they will amount to	31,050
Work-in-progress is likely to amount to at least three months' staff costs	9,000
Total Working Capital	£40,050

On these figures, inflation at 5 per cent. per annum would result in an increase in debtors and work in progress of about £2,000 but the partner's increased net profit would be only about £1,000. Thus not only would the partner be precluded (unless the firm borrowed) from withdrawing his additional profits, but he would be faced with finding an additional £1,000 working capital. If, in addition, a firm is growing in real terms this will impose a further working capital need and strain on distributable profits. All partnerships must from time to time therefore expect to face requirements for more capital at the expense of cash drawings. It is pressures such as these which require tight control over the use of working capital and in particular the need to send fees out regularly and collect debts quickly.

Credit Appraisal

Control is required, before the firm even makes its investment in a new assignment, in order to ensure that a bad credit risk is not taken on. This may come as something of a surprise to a professional practitioner, but the firm will sooner or later take on a client who proves unable to pay. To minimise the risk of this happening a procedure should be established by which potential new clients are assessed. That is not to suggest that each new client should be subjected to a credit vetting procedure such as might be adopted by a supplier of goods, but criteria need to be established which will identify those (probably few) clients where such a procedure is required. For many firms, new clients will come through recommendation and personal contact and the partner will feel confident that he is not going to be faced with a credit risk. But where the potential client is unknown as perhaps is the source of contact, there may well be a case for taking out references. The important point is that the firm should have agreed, and all the partners should be aware of, the circumstances when such vetting is to be carried out. An alternative procedure, commonly adopted where professional firms are asked to advise companies known to be in financial difficulties, is to ask for a payment in advance of the work carried out, perhaps on a weekly or monthly basis, thus reducing the risk of loss to the firm. But again, the firm must have agreed, and all the partners be aware of, the firm's policy on such cases.

Sending the Fee

Once the case has been taken on it is important that the firm's procedures are sufficiently well organised to keep the partner informed of when decisions on billing or cash collection should be considered by him. When the case is accepted and details entered into the firm's records the partner or fee earner should identify the expected date for billing and either a credit limit or at least a value of work-in-progress which, when reached, should be notified to him so that he can consider rendering an interim fee. As explained in Chapter 5, the work-in-progress records should be aged so that, whatever the amounts involved, the partner's attention can be drawn to those cases where there has been no movement on work in progress for, say, three months. Where time records are not maintained, such routines are difficult to achieve but the partner can at least be prompted if no fee has been rendered on a case that has been open for, say, six months or whatever interval is appropriate for the particular business. Similar information as to the age of disbursements expended on behalf of clients should be provided for each partner so that he can consider whether to request a payment on account.

Collecting the Cash

When the fee has been rendered, the firm's fee ledger should be maintained in such a way that outstanding balances can be aged. There should be a clear and well understood procedure for chasing fees. Some partners take exception to the firm's accounts department playing any part in this, arguing that they alone, being responsible to the firm for that client, should deal with such a sensitive matter as debt collection. Usually, however, it is not the best use of a partner's time for him to deal with the administrative aspects of debt collection, when, for many clients, all that is required to prompt payment is a standard letter of reminder which can be issued by the accounts department without prior reference to the partner. Furthermore, if a partner is out of the office a great deal or exceptionally busy or more likely prefers to spend his time on professional matters rather than collecting his debts, there may be unnecessary delay if it is left to him to take the initial step. The fact of the involvement of the firm's accounts department can also help maintain the necessary close relationship between the partner and his client in that the partner can, if appropriate, distance himself from the routine aspects of the debt collection procedure.

Ultimately, however, every partner must be prepared to deal direct with his client where payment has not been made in spite of one or more requests from the accounts department. Usually a telephone call is more effective than a letter for a client often has more difficulty in explaining his delay over the telephone than in correspondence. By the same token, in serious cases, a visit by the partner to the client may prove effective.

In extreme cases the firm may have to proceed to litigation, or the threat of it. If the firm's good name and reputation are to be maintained such action must be carefully controlled and there must be a clear process to be followed within the firm before instructions are issued to solicitors. Normally the prompting for such action should come from the accounts department but the decision to instruct lawyers must be taken by the partner himself. It is a good practice, on such occasions, if such a decision is referred by the partner responsible to another partner (perhaps the finance partner or managing partner) for a second opinion before the instructions are actually issued.

The commercial approach inherent in such procedures does not always sit easily with the professional approach that comes more naturally to the practitioner. But his firm is likely to be treated with greater respect by its clients if it displays a businesslike manner in these matters. If it does not it may also attract to it undesirable clients who will cause yet greater problems in the collection of fees. The partner must remember too that if the firm does not control its investment in work-in-progress and debtors, that will affect his own pocket by greater interest charges reducing his profits or, more noticeably, by an inability to withdraw his profits because the cash is not available. That will affect his partners as well as himself and those partners who find difficulty in dealing with clients who owe the firm money can sometimes be helped if a list of all overdue debts analysed by partner is circulated to all partners. As with deficits on fees rendered, most partners do not like to be seen to be out of step. If, in spite of that, certain partners still have an unacceptably high level of debtors, the direct involvement of the finance or managing partner may be appropriate.

Money Invested Outside the Firm

As well as capital locked up in work-in-progress and debtors, it is not unusual to find professional partnerships that have invested cash outside the business, perhaps in short-dated gilts or short term deposits, against the foreseen requirements to pay substantial liabilities, most usually taxation. Such investments directly increase the capital burden on partners. Yet when examined, it is common to find that when the tax bill or other liability falls due it has been paid not out of the proceeds of the ear-marked investment but out of the normal resources of the firm. Had the firm prepared cash projections it could probably have foreseen such an

eventuality and in that case have released the funds invested outside the firm, paid them back to partners and thus reduced the
level of capital demanded of partners. While caution is always
appropriate in such matters, most partners have no difficulty in
agreeing that it is better to have cash in their own hands than
locked up in the firm and, once again, provided there is adequate
financial control and forward planning, there are many occasions
when it is perfectly prudent to eliminate altogether such investments.

Sources of Capital

Even today there are many partners who subscribe to the view not
only that money should be invested outside the firm, as described
above, but that all of the capital requirements of the firm should be
put up by the partners. They therefore hesitate even to contemplate borrowing. In most firms however there will be quite marked
fluctuations in the level of working capital required, *e.g.* as work-
in-progress builds up and is then reduced by a burst of feeing or
when major items such as income tax or VAT are paid. It may also
be affected by seasonal factors. The result is that as well as the
hard core requirement for fixed and working capital there will be a
fluctuating demand for additional working capital. Provided the
firm has a good system of financial control and can adequately
forecast the likely level of its cash requirements, it is perfectly
appropriate for these temporary demands for working capital to be
financed by bank overdraft. Providing they can demonstrate to the
bank an adequate budgeting and cash forecasting capability, most
firms should have little difficulty in arranging an overdraft facility
of an amount at least equal to the total funds left in the business by
partners. If more permanent borrowed money is required, bank or
other loans can be considered, perhaps secured on insurance policies on the lives of the younger partners.

Undrawn Profits

Every successful firm will, of course, be generating profits as it
goes along and in most cases these will not be fully withdrawn
before the annual financial accounts are available. By that time,
further profits should have been earned in the new financial year,
and so the cycle continues. Undrawn profits are thus a very real
though often overlooked, source of capital. The use of service

companies as a vehicle in which to retain long term undrawn profits is discussed in Chapter 11.

Similarly, in any well managed firm, part of the profits will be set aside by way of a tax reserve which, until used, provides a further source of working capital for the business. Proper tax reserves are therefore an extremely important source of capital for most partnerships and can provide some of the extra capital required to cope with normal growth and inflation. Chapter 10 discusses fully the subject of tax reserves.

A number of other sources of capital may be mentioned. The subject of leasing has already been touched on and hire purchase may be a possibility. The decision on which source to use as compared with bank borrowings will naturally turn on both interest rates and availability of funds from the particular source. The possibilities should be re-examined each time any significant capital expenditure is proposed. For large firms with a substantial borrowing requirement, it may be possible to negotiate an acceptance credit facility or some other tailor-made arrangement at finer rates than are normally available for overdrafts. Finally, the credit taken from suppliers represents a source of capital. For most firms their major payments are salaries and wages in respect of which no credit can be taken. But even where suppliers are paid promptly there is still a delay between the date the goods or services are received and the date they are paid for. This contributes towards the firm's working capital, albeit in a partnership usually in a minor way.

If, in spite of the potential future difficulties for the partnership mentioned earlier in this chapter, the firm decides to invest in a genuinely fixed asset in the form of its office property, that must not be allowed to interfere with the firm's ability to generate adequate working capital. Unless the individual partners are persons of substance in their own right and can directly finance the acquisition, specific borrowing is likely to be required, no doubt secured on the property concerned. Any such borrowing should not be short term in nature. It is almost always a mistake to finance a long term asset out of short term borrowings; these should be restricted to the provision of working capital or other short term requirements.

Contribution of Capital by Partners

Whatever the efficiency of a firm in controlling its capital requirements, in most firms some level of permanent capital contribution will be required from partners. The exceptions may be firms that account on a cash basis and have therefore financed debtors and work-in-progress out of restricted earnings. It is desirable that this fixed capital should be contributed in profit sharing ratio. The capital is required solely to enable the firm to carry on business and earn profits and it is only equitable that those enjoying a larger share of those profits should put up a proportionally larger amount of capital.

Profits need not, of course, be divided on a simple percentage basis. Each partner may be credited first with a fixed sum as a notional salary, leaving only the balance to be divided in the profit sharing ratio. For simplicity the capital may still be contributed *pro rata* to that residual profit sharing ratio but the result is that the junior partner will have contributed proportionately less than the senior partner when compared with his total profit share including the notional salary. Normally that is correct and should not matter; if it causes concern, interest can be credited on capital accounts before applying the residual profit sharing ratios. Any adjustment to capital, increase or decrease, must of course be made in the same ratio in order to preserve the correct balance between partners.

While such a balance may be desirable it is not always achievable, at least in the short term. In many firms it is common to find that a disproportionate amount of capital has been contributed by senior partners. That too can be dealt with, from the point of view of equity, by crediting each partner with interest on capital as a prior charge on profits before the residue is divided in the profit sharing ratio. The greater difficulty comes when those partners wish to retire and withdraw their capital. It may be preferable, in such circumstances, to take steps before those retirements to adjust the balance of capital between partners. Thus if any capital can be repaid, it should go first to those who have contributed in excess of their profit share. If no repayments can be made then perhaps the more junior partners should increase their capital (out of withheld drawings) so that the senior partners shares can be reduced. Whilst that can be an emotive procedure, it at least gives the junior partners a longer period over which to make the adjustment than if the problem is only faced when the senior partners actually retire.

Most firms now compete for junior partners not only with each other but with commerce and industry. As few young professional men and women have substantial capital resources it is now common practice to allow them a period of a few years in which to build up their capital to the required level. This is normally done by retaining part of their profit share each year and, provided the capital requirements are not too onerous, it is a relatively painless process for the new partner. In the event that a partner (at whatever stage in his career) does have to borrow to meet his obligations to the firm, then the interest on such borrowings, if properly structured, will attract tax relief in the partner's hands.

Drawings

Most partnerships now accept that a clearly defined policy on partners' drawings is essential for the financial well-being not only of the firm but of the partners themselves. There are still some firms, however, where drawings are left to the discretion of the individual partners and rather more where the drawings, while controlled from the firm's point of view, are allowed to fluctuate markedly from month to month according to the short term cash needs of the business. Neither course can be recommended. If the procedures outlined earlier in this book for the efficient management of the cash resources of the business are followed, it is perfectly practicable to plan for a fixed level of drawings by partners each month. Both the firm and the individual partners can plan their cash flows accordingly.

The monthly drawings must of course be set at such a level that there is no risk of partners having drawn out, by the end of the year, more than their after-tax share of profits. The budgeted profits should therefore be taken as the starting point from which should be deducted a suitable allowance to cover contingencies. Allowance must then be made for taxation; for this purpose it is probably sufficient to assume an average rate of tax and apply it to the total of the profits. The resulting figure divided by 12 is then paid to partners each month as drawings. It is desirable that monthly drawings are not scaled precisely according to profit shares. They should either be the same for all partners or should only increase slightly according to profit shares. The result is that the more junior partners will take out a higher proportion of their entitlement as monthly drawings but that is normally appropriate as the financial demands on younger partners with young families are often proportionately greater than for the older partner, who will also have a larger final distribution of the previous year's profits to carry him through the following year.

The precise timing of the payment of the balance of profits to partners is a matter for decision by each firm according to its circumstances but the objective should be to pay partners out in full (after, of course, retaining tax reserves on whatever basis has been agreed) as soon as the annual financial accounts have been finalised and approved by partners. In practice it is to be hoped that

earlier drawings on account of the year's profit can be made at
intervals during the year. These should be based upon the results
revealed by the quarterly or half yearly accounts, again leaving a
fairly generous margin for contingencies. In addition, if the firm
has reserved for taxation on the basis recommended in Chapter 10
there may be surplus tax reserves to be released to partners each
year and the objective should be to pay these out to partners once
the reserves can be shown to be surplus to requirements. This will
normally be shortly after 6 April each year.

Thus for a firm drawing up financial accounts to 30 April each
year, an annual time-table for the withdrawal of profits (and surplus tax reserves, if applicable) could be as follows:

Monthly	drawings based on say 60 per cent. of budgeted after tax profits;
July	balance of previous year's profits based on approved annual accounts;
September	special drawings based on say 75 per cent. of profits shown by quarterly management accounts to July;
December	as for September special drawings, but based on October management accounts;
March	also as for September special drawings but based on January accounts;
May	withdrawal of any surplus tax reserves.

The timing of the special drawings can be adjusted to suit the
circumstances of the firm; it may, for example, be more appropriate to have a single such payment in December, based upon the
half year accounts. But the important point is that the timing of the
drawings should be planned in advance as part of the budgeting
and cash flow projections so that individual partners can make
their own plans with a reasonable degree of assurance that they
can rely on receiving drawings when they expect them.

If full payment of the profits to partners is not possible in respect
of any year, that eventuality should have been foreseen as part of
the planning process and partners alerted accordingly. And if that
withholding of profits is seen to be a permanent requirement then,
as explained above, the amount withheld should be credited to
partners' capital accounts and not, misleadingly, left on drawings
account.

Sometimes it is questioned whether a partner's share of the
firm's tax reserves should not be taken into account in assessing his
contribution to the required capital of the firm. Those tax reserves
will, as explained in Chapter 10, reflect the personal circumstances
of each partner. One partner may have fewer tax allowances than

another and thereby permanently leave in the firm a greater tax reserve than another; should he not be recompensed, in the form of interest on his tax reserves, by the firm which has benefited? There is a certain logical attraction to the argument, particularly if it is restricted to that part of the tax reserves which may, in due course, be released back to partners. But on the other hand, why should the personal circumstances of partners be taken into account in this way? Looked at from the point of view of the partner who takes full advantage of the retirement annuity policy rules and arranges his affairs to reduce his tax burden to the minimum, why should he be penalised by his own firm as a result? In addition, if the varying levels of tax reserves are to be taken into account in this way and, when they proportionately reduce for a partner, he is required to put in more capital or be charged interest, the mechanics become excessively complicated. This is one more example of there being no one correct answer. Probably in most circumstances it is unnecessary to go to the lengths of taking tax reserves into account in this way, but in exceptional circumstances some such adjustment may be desirable.

7 Clients' Money

Solicitors' clients have, for many years, enjoyed the statutory protection of having any money they may deposit with their solicitor placed in a client's bank account which is the subject of specific rules and an independent accountant's review. Similar regulations have more recently been introduced in respect of clients' money held by chartered surveyors but other professions, not covered by such rules, also commonly hold clients' money. This chapter therefore sets out some of the general principles required to be followed by solicitors and estate agents, since these represent no more than best practice which should be followed by all firms holding clients' money. In any case, investor protection legislation seems likely to require all firms to follow similar principles in future.

It should be remembered that in the case of solicitors and chartered surveyors each partner is individually responsible for the firm's proper custody of clients' money and that a breach of the rules by one partner or fee-earner or by the accounts department is the responsibility of every partner in the firm. Responsibility and accountability for clients' funds cannot be delegated. But even where there is no sanction such as is imposed by the Solicitors Accounts Rules or the Royal Institution of Chartered Surveyors Members Accounts Regulations, any mishandling of clients monies will redound to the detriment of the whole firm and each partner and fee-earner should therefore be fully aware of and comply with the procedures laid down by the firm.

Clients' Accounts

Any clients' money received by the firm must be banked without delay in a separate bank account designated as a clients' account. Without delay means on the day of receipt, or the next day if received after banking hours. The inclusion of the word "client" in the title of the account is important. In its absence it may not be clear that the firm or its creditors does not have title to the money; banks, for instance, may be able to claim set off against other accounts if it is not clear that the money is held in a clients' account. Should a cheque be received which contains both clients' money and money due to the firm it must first be banked in the clients' account and the office element then transferred into the firm's own bank account.

Solicitors and chartered surveyors are subject to specific restrictions as to the organisations with which they can place clients' money. Broadly these are officially recognised banks and the Post Office; they do not include investment institutions or any organisation not directly carrying on banking in the accepted sense of the word or, in the case of solicitors, building societies. While other professions are not subject to these restrictions the firm must obviously have regard to the fact that it is being entrusted with the responsibility for clients' money and it should judge accordingly the standing of the organisation which it proposes to use. Furthermore, in the absence of instructions to the contrary, the money must be readily available; if placed on deposit therefore it should be withdrawable on demand or short notice. The client's instructions are of course paramount, and even where there are regulations governing the application of clients' money these must be over-ridden if the client so instructs. The firm should take care, however, to ensure that the client puts his instructions in writing or should itself confirm in writing its understanding of those instructions.

Money held by a firm as stakeholder is not strictly clients' money. Nevertheless, it is good practice to account for it in a separately designated account and to apply the same controls over withdrawal as the firm applies to clients' accounts.

Money in a solicitor's or chartered surveyor's clients' account may be utilised for the following principal purposes:

— to meet the express instructions of the client;
— to effect a transfer of money that should not have been paid into the clients' account;
— to meet the practitioner's fee, provided that the fee has been delivered to the client and he has been told, in writing, that the money is to be applied for that purpose;
— to cover expenses incurred by the practitioner on behalf of the client;
— to effect a transfer to another client account; again care should be taken to ensure that such transfers are supported by written instructions.

Firms in other professions should seek to follow similar practices. Only practising solicitors or legal executives meeting certain requirements are allowed to sign cheques drawn on solicitors' clients' accounts and somewhat similar rules apply to chartered surveyors. For other professions it will normally be appropriate to limit such signing powers solely to partners.

Interest

Solicitors and chartered surveyors are empowered by statute to retain in certain circumstances interest on clients' money placed on a general deposit account. They must, however, normally account to clients for interest on monies in excess of £500 deposited with them and which, in the case of solicitors' clients, at the time of receipt were unlikely to be disbursed or reduced to below £500 within two months.

Maintenance of Records

It is obviously crucial to ensure that accurate and up to date records of clients' monies are maintained by the firm. These should be subject to the firm's normal internal control so that those responsible for maintenance of the records have no authority over the direction of the monies in the account. The total held on clients' account must be regularly (at least three monthly for solicitors and chartered surveyors) reconciled with the balances on the clients' account at the bank. It should be the responsibility of the finance partner to see that this is carried out. Solicitors are required to keep all supporting documentation (which includes returned cheques) for at least six years; other firms should normally follow the same policy.

8 The Partnership Income Tax Assessment

It is inevitable that in any sophisticated business the taxation aspects of particular transactions will assume a degree of importance, and tax planning will become a regular feature of the commercial life of the firm. It is essential therefore, for partners to have a basic understanding of the rules of taxation so far as they affect the partnership's affairs.

The profits attributable to individual partners in a partnership are subject to income tax; corporation tax is only applicable to a corporate partner's share of a partnership's income or to profits which may be retained by a firm's service company. The professional income of a firm attributable to the individual as distinct from corporate partners is liable to income tax under Schedule D Case II, and it is with this income that this chapter is primarily concerned. Investment income of the firm is taxable under different heads and is discussed below in Chapter 9. Case I of Schedule D applies to income from trades; Case II to income from professions and vocations. In some instances, perhaps most notably stock-broking, the distinction between a trade and profession is somewhat blurred, but in any event this is of no consequence since the rules of assessment for Cases I and II are identical.

Income tax is levied by reference to fiscal years, which are years commencing on 6 April and ending on the following 5 April. Since very few professional firms make up accounts to 5 April each year, it will be apparent that there need to be special rules for assessing partnership income. These rules are complex, but there is one fundamental rule which it is important to grasp. The rule is that tax is not paid *on* partnership profits but *by reference to* partnership profits. Once that concept is grasped, then it becomes easier to understand both the normal rules of assessment and the special rules attributable to the opening and closing years of a partnership.

Some partners find it difficult to appreciate that they are paying tax in any fiscal year on profits which they may or may not have enjoyed themselves. For example, a new partner joining a well established firm will pay tax in the first year of his partnership by reference to profits which were actually enjoyed by other people.

Similarly, some find it difficult to accept that a partner will enjoy profits in the last year of his partnership and then retire leaving others to pay the tax by reference to those profits. This is why it is important to understand that tax is paid by reference to profits rather than on profits. A partner need not concern himself with who enjoyed the profits by reference to which he is paying tax; his only concern is to compare the profits he is actually enjoying with those by reference to which he is having to pay tax. If profits are rising year by year, that comparison will always be in his favour.

The Normal Basis of Assessment

An established partnership will pay tax for any fiscal year by reference to the profits earned in its accounting year which ended in the preceding fiscal year. Thus, such a partnership will pay tax in 1986/87 by reference to profits earned in its accounting year which ended between 6 April 1985 and 5 April 1986. Thus for 1986/87, some firms will be paying tax by reference to profits earned as early as the year ended 30 April 1985, while others will be paying tax by reference to profits earned in the year to 31 March 1986. The full significance of the accounting date will be explored below. This normal basis of assessment is frequently referred to as the preceding year basis of assessment—for obvious reasons.

The Commencement Provisions

It will be apparent, however, that such a basis of assessment cannot be applied to a new firm since there will be no previous accounting period the profits of which can be used as a basis of assessment. The rules of assessment are therefore adapted to cater for these special circumstances. Thus the profits taxable for the fiscal year in which a business commences are those profits which are strictly attributable on a time basis to that fiscal year. For example, if a business commenced on 1 October 1985 and made up its first accounts to 30 September 1986, the profits assessable in 1985/86 would be the proportion of the first year's profits which were attributed on a time basis to the period from 1 October 1985 to 5 April 1986. The legislation requires this apportionment to be done on the basis of months and fractions of months. Frequently however, the apportionment is done simply on a daily basis.

The second year of assessment in this example would be 1986/87, and once again there is no basis period (to use the technical term) of an accounting year ended in the previous fiscal year. The rules therefore stipulate that the assessment for the second fiscal year of the partnership shall be based on the profits attributable to the first year's activity of the new firm. In the example, the firm made up its accounts for a period of exactly one year from the date of commencement, and therefore the assessment for 1986/87 will be based on the profits of the year ended 30 September 1986. If, however, the first accounts had been made up to a date more or less than one year from the date of commencement, the second year's assessment would have been based on an apportionment of exactly twelve months' profits from either the first accounting period (if that period was in excess of twelve months) or from the first and then, to the extent necessary, from the second accounting periods if the first accounting period was shorter than a full year.

By the time the third year of assessment is reached, the business that made up its first account for a period of exactly one year can move on to the normal preceding year basis of assessment. In the example, the profits of the year ended 30 September 1986 will constitute a normal basis period for the 1987/88 assessment on the firm, and thereafter the normal preceding year basis of assessment will apply. For the firm whose first accounts were not for a period of exactly one year, however, the requirement for there to be a period of account *of exactly one year* ended in the previous fiscal year will still not apply for 1987/88, and it is the Inland Revenue's normal practice for the profits to be assessed in the third year to be the same profits as were assessed in the second year. For such firms, it is not until the fourth year of assessment that the normal preceding year basis can be seen to apply.

The opening rules of assessment will give the impression that some of the profits earned in the first year of operation to 30 September 1986 will be taxed three times over. More strictly, the position is that the assessments for the first three fiscal years of the new business are calculated in part *by reference to* the same profits. The profits of the period from 1 October 1985 to 5 April 1986 form all or part of the assessment for 1985/86, 1986/87 and 1987/88. This, it would seem, is distinctly unfair on the taxpayer. Normally speaking, however, this is not the case. In practice, the profits of the first year of a new business are likely to be lower than those earned in the second and subsequent years. It would be an unusual business that engages top gear in its first trading period. A more normal pattern would be for the first year to reflect low profits or, possibly, losses as the business gets under way and begins to establish itself. Thus it is not a hardship for the income tax assessment in the second and third years of a new business to be based on the profits of the first year since this would normally mean that tax is being paid for those years by reference to lower profits than are in fact being enjoyed by the partners. Even if this ideal pattern did not work out in practice, the taxpayers' position is safeguarded by an election available to them whereby at any time within seven years after the end of the second year of assessment, the partners may elect for the assessments for the second and third years of the partnership to be based on the actual profits apportioned to those fiscal years rather than by reference to the special rules of assessment outlined above.

The Discontinuance Provisions

Whilst the partners are put into a position whereby some of the profits of the first year of business form the basis of assessment for two or three years of assessment, the position is reversed when the business finally comes to an end. The operation of the rules of assessment appropriate in that instance mean that some of the profits earned by the partnership do not form the basis of any assessment to income tax. The special rules appropriate on the discontinuance of a business can be summarised as follows. Tax will be payable for the last year of assessment during which the partnership is trading by reference to the profits apportioned to the period from 6 April in the year of discontinuance to the date of discontinuance. Thus to continue the example (and assuming the law remains unchanged), if the firm ceased to trade on 31 December 1992, the last year of assessment would be 1992/93 and the assessment for that year would be based on the profits apportioned to the period from 6 April 1992 to 31 December 1992 out of the profits for the year ended 30 September 1992 plus the profits earned in the period from 1 October to 31 December 1992. There are then special rules which apply to the assessments for the two previous fiscal years, namely 1990/91 and 1991/92. Originally, the assessments for these two years would have been based on the profits of the firm for its years ended 30 September 1989 and 1990, but the Inspector of Taxes has the right to base the 1990/91 and 1991/92 assessments on the actual profits apportioned to those fiscal years. He would thus take the appropriate portions from the firm's accounting years ended 30 September 1990, 1991 and 1992. The Inspector will revise the assessments for the two years concerned (and he cannot revise one year and not the other) if by doing so he will increase the gross assessments for those years.

Since in these circumstances the assessments for 1990/91 and 1991/92 can be based on the profits of either the two years ended 30 September 1990 or the two years ended 5 April 1992, it will be apparent that the profits of a period of approximately a year and a half will not form the basis of any assessment. Thus if the assessments are left on the preceding year basis the profits of the period from 1 October 1990 to 5 April 1992 will not form the basis of any assessment, whereas if the assessments are revised to tax the actual profits attributable to 1990/91 and 1991/92, the profits of the period from 1 October 1988 to 5 April 1990 will not form the basis of any assessment. In this way, equity is seen to be achieved. The profits of the first year of the new business formed the basis of assessment for an extra one and a half times, while the profits of one and a half years towards the end of the trading cycle of the business do not form the basis of any assessment. However, as was suggested earlier, the rules of assessment can be expected to act in the taxpayer's favour since it is reasonably likely that the profits of the business in later years will be larger than those of the first year. Profits which escape assessment can be expected to be greater than those which form the basis of more than one assessment.

The Choice of Accounting Date

A full appreciation of the normal impact of the rules of assessment of partnership profits will demonstrate the advantage that can be secured by choosing an accounting date which ends early rather than late in the fiscal year. Thus it is better for a firm to make up its accounts to, say, 30 April in each year than 31 March. There are two principal reasons for this. Firstly, while profits are rising this will give the "April" firm a cash flow advantage over the "March" firm, since the interval is longer between the earning of profits and the time at which tax is paid by reference to those profits. Secondly, if profits increase year by year, maximum benefit will be gained from the preceding year basis of assessment. This is probably most clearly illustrated by means of a simple example, as follows:

Two identical firms commence business around the end of March/beginning of April 1985 and make up annual accounts to 31 March/30 April each year until 1991 when the business ceases. The profits earned in these six accounting years are as follows:

		£
Year to 31 March/30 April	1986	80,000
	1987	150,000
	1988	200,000
	1989	220,000
	1990	250,000
	1991	275,000

Applying the appropriate rules of assessment outlined in the previous paragraphs, and ignoring for the moment the cessation rules, the assessments raised on the two firms (ignoring the strict apportionment of profits to the short periods from 1–5 April and 6–30 April respectively) are as follows:

	"March" firm	*"April" firm*
	£	£
1984/85	NIL	(Not applicable)
1985/86	80,000	80,000
1986/87	80,000	80,000
1987/88	150,000	80,000
1988/89	200,000	150,000
1989/90	220,000	200,000
1990/91	250,000	220,000
	£980,000	£810,000

It will be seen from the above figures that by the time both firms are well established on the normal preceding year basis—for example in 1988/89—the amount of profits being assessed on the April firm is considerably less than that being assessed on the March firm. By delaying the year end by merely one month—but a month which spans the end of a fiscal year—a considerable cash flow advantage is achieved for the April firm since the profits assessed on the normal preceding year basis for any fiscal year are those of nearly a whole year earlier (*e.g.* the year to April 1987 rather than to March 1988). Moreover, this cash flow advantage increases year by year if profits continue to rise, and it will be seen from the above figures that by 1990/91 the March firm will have paid tax by reference to profits of £980,000 whereas the April firm will have paid tax on profits of only £810,000.

The sceptical observer is unable to deny the apparent advantage gained by the April firm at that stage, but believes that the advantage is only temporary and that "it will catch up with you in the end." This is only partially true; in addition to the cash flow advantage which accrues when profits are rising, there is normally an absolute advantage in having an April accounting date. In the foregoing example, once the firms continue trading beyond 5 April 1990, there is no way open to the Inspector of Taxes of revising the 1987/88 assessment to tax the actual profits attributable to that year, and the assessment is irrevocably determined on the preceding year basis. This means that although in the year to March/April 1988 while the firms were earning £200,000, the March firm for the corresponding fiscal year of 1987/88 paid tax on £150,000 while the April firm paid tax on only £80,000. Both firms have therefore secured an advantage, but the advantage accruing to the April firm is much the more significant.

Let us now consider the operation of the discontinuance rules. If the firms decided to cease business at the termination of their accounting years ending March/April 1991, the Inspector has the right to exercise the option available to him described above. The March firm will have ceased trading in the fiscal year 1990/91, and the assessment for that year will therefore be based on the profits earned in the year, namely £275,000 (approximately). Furthermore, the Inspector will exercise his option for the two previous fiscal years of 1988/89 and 1989/90 and revise the assessments to £220,000 and £250,000 respectively. Over the whole lifetime of the March partnership, the profits earned and the profits assessed will therefore be as follows:

	Profits earned £	Profits assessed £
1985/86	80,000	80,000
1986/87	150,000	80,000
1987/88	200,000	150,000
1988/89	220,000	220,000
1989/90	250,000	250,000
1990/91	275,000	275,000
	£1,175,000	£1,055,000

By contrast the April firm will have continued trading just into 1991/92 (making profits which we have assumed will be nil) so that the Inspector has the right to look back under the discontinuance rules to 1989/90 and 1990/91. The comparative figures for the April firm then become:

	Profits earned	Profits assessed
	£	£
1985/86	80,000	80,000
1986/87	150,000	80,000
1987/88	200,000	80,000
1988/89	220,000	150,000
1989/90	250,000	250,000
1990/91	275,000	275,000
1991/92	Nil	Nil
	£1,175,000	£915,000

The relative benefits enjoyed by the two firms can be explained in terms of a comparison of the profits which did not form the basis of assessment (or, for simplicity were not assessed) on the discontinuance with those which were assessed more than once on commencement. In the case of the March firm, the profits not assessed were those for 1987/88, namely £200,000 compared with the profits of 1985/86 of £80,000 which were assessed twice—a net benefit of £120,000. By contrast, the April firm had the profits of nearly two years not forming the basis of any assessment—namely the £420,000 of the two years to April 1989—compared with the profits of 1985/86 of £80,00 being assessed twice over. The benefit enjoyed by this firm was thus £420,000 less £160,000, namely £260,000. The overall benefit gained by having an April accounting date—or at the very least one which ends earlier rather than later in the fiscal year—is irrefutable.

Changing the Accounting Date

The accounting date of many firms will have been chosen in a purely random fashion. The calendar year is a natural choice, in the absence of any strong indicator that the date is inappropriate and, despite it being a most inappropriate date, there is evidence that the accounting date of 40 per cent. of unincorporated businesses is 31 March. Certainly over 50 per cent. of professional firms have accounting dates which fall in the second half of the fiscal year, and it would be hard if, as a result of a random choice, such firms were for ever to be penalised. However, it is possible for a firm to change its permanent accounting date, and thereby move to one which gives more of the advantages which have been outlined. If a firm wishes to move its accounting date from September to April, for example, this could be achieved by means of a seven month or a 19 month accounting period. In either event, the short or long accounting period would deny the operation of the normal preceding year basis of assessment since there would not be a twelve month period of account as a basis period for a subsequent year of assessment. In such circumstances, there has to be some sort of compromise arrangement and the procedure normally adopted by the Inland Revenue in these circumstances is set out in their explanatory booklet IR26, entitled "Changes of accounting date."

The objective of the Revenue's procedure can, on reflection, be appreciated. As was demonstrated in the foregoing examples, on a discontinuance of a firm with an April accounting date, the profits of nearly two years do not form the basis of any assessment, and this compares with a similar period of only approximately one year for a firm with a March accounting date. A partnership with a September accounting date would fall midway between those two extremes, with the profits of approximately 18 months not coming into assessment on a discontinuance. If the Inland Revenue are to countenance a firm moving to a position where potentially the profits of a longer period would fall out of assessment on a discontinuance, they will naturally want to be compensated, and this compensation comes through the double assessment of the profits of a further period—of nearly six months in the case of a move from a September to an April accounting date. The calculations involved in working out the assessments for the affected years on a change of accounting date are moderately complicated and need not be described in full here. The principle involved is for the profits of the period immediately prior to the change in the permanent accounting date to be averaged and the average rate of profit over the affected period of, say, 31 or 43 months (in the case of a move from a September to an April account date) to be applied to give the assessments for the longer period of three or four years respectively. A small, once-off, advantage, in the form of a reduction in the assessment for one year, can sometimes be achieved on a firm changing its accounting date but, what is more important, the more permanent advantages of an accounting date ending early in the fiscal year can then be expected.

It should be stressed that changing a firm's accounting date does not trigger a discontinuance for tax purposes, neither does it give the Inland Revenue the ability to require the partnership to change the basis on which it draws up accounts. Thus the fears of some that a cash or bills issued basis of accounting will be lost if the firm changes its accounting date, are ill-founded.

While all the implications for assessments following a change of accounting date should be fully considered in advance, the Inland

Revenue, not unreasonably, may not take kindly to a change of accounting date which has been made retrospectively once the profits earned after the proposed new permanent accounting date have been determined.

Partnership Changes

This chapter so far has talked in terms of the initial commencement of a partnership and its ultimately ceasing to trade. However, these are not the only occasions when special rules of assessment may apply. The Taxes Acts currently regard any change in the composition of a partnership (but not a mere change in the proportions in which profits are shared) as the discontinuance of the existing firm and the commencement of a new firm. When that occurs, the closing rules of assessment already described come into effect, while some different rules—described below—apply to the "new" firm.

It will be realised from the discussion earlier in the chapter that, when profits are rising, the effect of a discontinuance could be to increase very considerably the assessments for two or three years and, if that result inevitably followed from the admission of a new partner, this could impose a very serious barrier to the introduction of new blood into a partnership. However, a procedure is available whereby the partnership can elect for the change in the composition of the partnership to be ignored for tax purposes and for the assessments to continue on the preceding year basis. The election, commonly known as a continuation election must be signed by all the partners in the firm immediately preceding and following the partnership change or changes. Thus, retiring partners and new partners as well as the continuing partners must sign the election and lodge it with the Inspector of Taxes within two years of the date of the partnership change. The Inland Revenue like to know the partners' intentions with regard to partnership changes just as soon as possible, and they therefore encourage the submission of a continuation election at an early stage. However, by an unpublished concession, they will permit the revocation of a continuation election as long as that revocation is also signed by all the relevant partners and submitted within the same two year period.

As will be explained later, a continuation election will be submitted for most partnership changes and it will be in only special circumstances that it will be in the partners' interests for the firm to be treated as discontinued on the occasion of a partnership change. This is because the "recommencement provisions" introduced by the Finance Act 1985 afford a much less favourable treatment to the "new" firm which commences after the deemed discontinuance than was the position up to 19 March 1985. For partnership changes that occurred prior to 20 March 1985, the normal discontinuance and commencement rules already described came into effect. Under the old regime, therefore, it was sometimes advantageous for a firm to allow a partnership change which took place at the beginning of what transpired to be a poor year to be treated as a discontinuance for tax purposes, so that the profits of that poor year formed the basis of the assessment for that year and the following two years.

In order to counteract that advantage, the Finance Act 1985 introduced the recommencement rules to apply following a discontinuance on or after 20 March 1985. These rules provide that the assessments for the year of recommencement and the following three fiscal years shall all be based on the actual profits attributable to those years. The normal preceding year basis does not apply until the fifth and sixth years of assessment, although the taxpayer has the right to elect for the profits of those two years also to be based on the years' actual profits. This election is similar to the election available for the second and third years of a genuine new business.

If an established partnership now has a discontinuance for tax purposes, this will mean that the profits of six consecutive years are likely to be assessed on an actual basis. It has been demonstrated earlier that, with rising profits, the preceding year basis of assessment can give rise to significant tax savings, and therefore the prospect of six years without the possibility of making any tax savings is a relatively unattractive one. Indeed, partnerships may prefer to suffer for one or two years in which tax is paid on amounts in excess of the earnings for those years so as to preserve for themselves the possibility of earning profits in excess of those being assessed for the other four or five years out of the six years otherwise affected by the discontinuance. It is for this reason that a discontinuance is likely to be relatively rare and will probably only be countenanced if profits are regularly declining year by year. For such a business, the tax position is unlikely to be the partners' only worry!

If for the sake of partners of other years, partners of one or two years are asked to pay tax on amounts in excess of their earnings, it would be fair and reasonable for those partners to be compensated by the partners of the other years who hoped to gain by avoiding a discontinuance. It would be fair for what are known as "equity adjustments" to be effected whereby those who stand to gain from the continuation election compensate those who suffer. These equity adjustments are facilitated if tax reserves retained within the partnership are adequate to meet the firm's tax liabilities on either the preceding year or actual bases. Indeed the recommencement rules emphasise the importance for a partnership to have a proper policy for the establishment of tax reserves within the partnership accounts; this subject is discussed more fully in Chapter 10.

The new recommencement rules do not apply to the smallest partnership. If one partner of a two partner firm retires, and a continuation election is not submitted, the remaining partner effectively becomes a sole trader. In those circumstances, the normal commencement rules apply to his new business rather than the recommencement rules. Similarly, if a sole trader takes in a partner and does not elect for continuation treatment, the new, two-man partnership is subject to the commencement rather than the recommencement rules. This is thus an important relief for the small partnership.

The Division of the Assessment

If the first difficult concept to grasp in relation to partnership taxation is that tax is paid by reference to profits rather than on profits, the second concept which often gives rise to considerable confusion is the manner in which the assessment on the firm is divided between the partners. A grasp of this aspect is therefore essential to a full understanding of the basis of partnership tax.

The first step in calculating the tax payable by a partnership for any year is to determine the extent of the taxable profit on the appropriate basis—*i.e.* either the preceding year or actual basis. From this "gross" assessment will be deducted the partnership's entitlement to capital allowances, if any. The resulting "net" figure is the net assessment which is divisible between the partners "according to their interests during the year of assessment." In simpler English, this means that the assessment for any fiscal year is divided between the partners of that fiscal year in the same manner as the partners divide between themselves the actual profits being earned *during* the fiscal year. However, except in a static partnership, it is likely that two different sets of profit sharing arrangements will have been in force during any fiscal year. Thus for a firm which makes up its accounts to 30 September, the 1985/86 fiscal year will be affected by the profit sharing arrangements which applied for the years ended 30 September 1985 and 1986. However, the principle governing the division of the assessment must be strictly adhered to, and therefore the 1985/86 assessment will be divided on a time apportionment basis to cover firstly the period from 6 April to 30 September 1985 and secondly 1 October 1985 to 5 April 1986. The profit sharing arrangements which applied in those two accounting periods will then be applied to the part of the assessment apportioned to each period. For example:

XYZ & Co. make up accounts to 5 July each year. Z has a prior charge on the profits by way of salary of £10,000 before the profits are divided as to:

	Year ended 5 July	
	1985	*1986*
	%	%
X	40	35
Y	40	35
Z	20	30
	100	100

The tax adjusted profits for the year ended 5 July 1984 were £110,000. The assessment for 1985/86 is divided as follows:

	6 April–5 July 1985			*6 July 1985–5 April 1986*			
	Salary	*Balance*	*Total*	*Salary*	*Balance*	*Total*	*TOTAL*
X	—	10,000	10,000	—	26,250	26,250	36,250
Y	—	10,000	10,000	—	26,250	26,250	36,250
Z	2,500	5,000	7,500	7,500	22,500	30,000	37,500
	2,500	25,000	27,500	7,500	75,000	82,500	£110,000

Once the net assessment has been divided between the partners in this manner each partner's personal tax allowances and reliefs are set against his share of the assessment to establish his share of the firm's overall tax liability for the year. Thus although tax is payable by the firm on a single assessment, the actual tax payable is calculated by reference to the circumstances of each individual partner for the particular year of assessment. The tax assessed is payable in two instalments which in principle should be equal, on 1 January in the year of assessment and on the following 1 July.

9 Capital Allowances and the Taxation of Other Partnership Income and Gains

The previous chapter discussed briefly the rules by which income assessable under Schedule D Cases I and II is assessed. The profits which are assessed under those rules or are apportioned to fiscal years to be assessed on an actual basis are the tax adjusted profits after the various adjustments required by the Taxes Acts have been made. A full commentary on all the adjustments which are likely to be made in arriving at the profits for tax purposes is not appropriate for this book, but a brief summary is required in order to appreciate the significance of capital allowances.

The Tax Computation

The starting point for a tax computation is the profit divisible between the equity partners. This profit will include any amounts paid by way of "salary" or "interest" to equity partners as prior shares of profit. These prior shares are not expenses of the business, but merely part of the way in which the partners have decided to allocate the profit between themselves. The salary and bonus (if any) of the salaried partners will have been taxed on those partners under Schedule E and are an expense of the business and will be charged before arriving at the profit divisible between the equity partners. To that profit must be added those items of expenditure which have been charged against the profit but which, through specific direction of the Taxes Acts are not "allowable" for tax purposes. Thus expenditure which is primarily for the personal benefit of the partners (such as permanent health and life insurance), the cost of business entertaining of UK clients, items of a capital as distinct from revenue nature and so on are added back in the computation of the Case I or II profit. Depreciation, or the writing off of fixed assets, is similarly not an allowable deduction for tax purposes and must be added back, though a broadly corresponding deduction will normally be available by way of capital allowances. Income which does not form part of the normal professional earnings of the firm, and in particular investment income in the form of bank or building society interest and dividends on stocks and shares is deducted from the professional earnings (as adjusted) and taxed in a different way. The end result of all these adjustments is to arrive at a figure for the tax adjusted professional earnings perhaps on the following lines:

			£
Profit (including partners' salaries, etc.) attributable to the equity partners			200,000
Add:	Depreciation	35,000	
	UK entertaining	2,500	
	Legal expenses (*e.g.* re new lease)	500	
	Sundry expenses	1,000	
			39,000
			239,000
Less:	Bank deposit interest		9,000
Case II profit			£230,000

It is this tax adjusted figure which falls to be dealt with on the normal preceding year basis or by the rules of assessment for the opening and closing years of a partnership.

The figure on which the partners ultimately have to pay tax will, however, probably be significantly less than the Case II profit. This is because there are available to partners certain other allowances and reliefs which are deducted before the net amount is charged to tax. The principal deduction to be described briefly is for capital allowances. Stock relief, a deduction based on the value of the firm's stock or work in progress was available for years whose assessments were based on the profits of accounting periods up to and including 12 March 1984. Stock relief was abolished for any inflationary increase in the value of stock after that date, and events occurring subsequent to 12 March 1984 will not trigger a clawback of stock relief previously granted.

Capital Allowances

Capital allowances are the allowances granted for expenditure on certain items of a capital nature. Broadly speaking, most of the capital expenditure incurred by professional offices will be on items which fall within the general heading of "plant and machinery" and includes office furniture and fittings and office machinery such as computers, typewriters, calculators and so on. Normally speaking, expenditure on extending or improving the office premises will not qualify for capital allowances. Plant and machinery is currently eligible for a first year allowance and then writing down allowances, but first year allowances are being phased out and are not available for expenditure incurred after 31 March 1986. For plant and machinery acquired in the year before 31 March 1986, a first year allowance of 50 per cent. was granted for the accounting period in which the expenditure was incurred, with the balance of the tax allowance being granted for successive years at 25 per cent. per annum on the written down balance brought forward.

In practice, expenditure on individual items of plant and machinery is not separately identified, but is lumped together in a "pool" and the writing down allowance is calculated in a single sum. When items of plant and machinery are sold, the sales proceeds are credited against the pool so as to reduce the written down value ("WDV") carried forward, and thereby the writing down allowance ("WDA") available for that and subsequent accounting periods.

For expenditure incurred after 31 March 1986, as no separate first year allowance is available, the 25 per cent. per annum writing down allowance will commence in the year of acquisition. This system is similar to the basis which has applied for a number of years of granting capital allowance for expenditure on motor cars. A first year allowance has never been available for motor cars and the 25 per cent. writing down allowance has been limited to a maximum of £2,000 per annum. "Expensive" cars, which are still defined in statute as those costing more than £8,000, thus do not attract a full 25 per cent. writing down allowance until the WDV is below £8,000. Until that time, the allowance is restricted to £2,000 per annum. For this reason, it is necessary in the tax computation to identify separately "expensive" cars, so that the appropriate WDA can be calculated.

When such a car is sold, the proceeds are compared with the WDV brought forward at the beginning of the year during which the disposal took place, and a balancing allowance (where the proceeds were less than the WDV) or a balancing charge (where the proceeds exceeded the WDV) is calculated. This balancing adjustment is then added to or subtracted from the other capital allowances calculated by reference to the accounting period concerned. It will be appreciated that, although the WDA may be restricted during the early years of the ownership of an expensive car, tax relief for the whole of the difference between the cost and the resale proceeds will ultimately be received, even if only by way of a balancing allowance in the year in which the disposal takes place.

The principal difference between the relief secured by means of capital allowances and the normal expenses of the business is that tax relief for the former is secured for the partners once and once only. By contrast, expenses charged in arriving at the tax adjusted profit may effectively attract tax relief two or more times or not at all depending on whether they were charged against the profits of accounting periods affected by the opening and closing rules of assessment. Capital allowances are deducted from the taxable profit for the appropriate year of assessment once that assessment has been determined on the appropriate basis (*i.e.* the preceding year or actual basis). Thus in terms of tax planning and the decision whether or not to treat a partnership change as a discontinuance of the firm for tax purposes, capital allowances are not relevant. The fundamental question of whether or not relief is secured is not affected by a discontinuance; the relief is certain.

A discontinuance for tax purposes will normally result in a "bunching" of capital allowances. Thus in a normal continuing business, relief for capital allowances will be granted on the preceding year basis—that is a year or two in arrears. On a discontinuance, there is a catching up. By the date of the discontinuance, full relief will be granted for all capital allowances due up to that date, and this means that in one year of assessment there will be relief for first year allowances relating to expenditure on plant and machinery over two or three accounting years. The actual rules are moderately complicated and will not be discussed in detail here; suffice it to say that a discontinuance can enable an acceleration of tax relief for expenditure on plant and machinery.

Charges on Income

The other item of tax relief which deserves a separate brief mention is the category of charges on income. These items are difficult to define though normally easy to recognise. The common link between most charges on income is the fact that they are partnership outgoings that are paid under deduction of tax at source. The most common charges on income for partnerships are annuities to retired partners, charitable covenants and, in certain circumstances interest paid under deduction of income tax at basic rate. A deduction for these charges is not allowed in arriving at the adjusted Case I/II profit, but tax relief is secured for each partner in a slightly different form though the end result is broadly similar.

He effectively obtains relief at the basic rate by retaining his share of the tax deducted at source. If a partner pays tax at higher rates, his share of the charges is deducted in arriving at his income for higher tax purposes.

The main difference occasioned by charges on income is the timing of the tax relief. Relief for charges on income is granted in the fiscal year during which the payment is actually made. Thus payments made between 6 April 1986 and 5 April 1987 will attract tax relief in 1986/87 even though most of the profits of that period may form the basis of assessment for a different year. Thus it can be seen that tax relief for charges paid is secured considerably earlier than relief for the normal expenses of the business.

The Taxation of Other Income

It is not appropriate to discuss in any great detail the basis of taxation of a firm's non-professional income, or its capital gains. This book does not set out to be a general textbook on income tax, but it is merely worth noting that the existence of a partnership does not affect the basis of assessing the investment income which accrues to individual partners via the partnership. While the assessment of the firm's professional earnings is raised in one figure on the partnership itself, assessments are raised on the partners individually for each partner's share of the firm's other income and capital gains. Thus for example, a partner's share in the firm's investment income is treated as a separate source of income for each partner subject to assessment under the applicable rules. It follows that, if a partner has a share in the firm's taxed investment income, he may expect a demand, if appropriate, for income tax at higher rates in respect of his share of that income.

The most common form of investment income for a partnership is interest earned on the firm's bank deposit accounts. Since 5 April 1985, this bank deposit interest has, in the main, been paid under deduction of tax at source, so that partners are liable only for tax on this income at higher rates. Bank deposit interest earned on some partnership deposits continues to be paid gross. Most commonly, this will be interest paid to solicitors on a clients' general deposit account, and interest paid to a partnership which contains a corporate partner. This income will thus be assessable on the partners under the general rules for the taxation of income under Schedule D Case III, which has its own commencement rules. When an individual is admitted to a partnership in receipt of gross interest, and he therefore starts to share in that interest, the new partner is deemed to have acquired a fresh source of income thereby bringing into play the commencement rules of assessment, even though the remaining partners continue to be assessed on the preceding year basis in relation to what is, for them, a continuing source of income.

For example, a new partner is admitted on 1 May 1986 and receives a share in the firm's gross interest income for the year to 30 April 1987 of £1,000 out of £10,000 (all of which is assumed to have been earned in the 1986/87 fiscal year). His £1,000 will form the basis of assessment for 1986/87 while the £9,000 accruing to the other partners will form the basis of assessment on them in 1987/88.

The same logic applies when a partner retires. He is regarded as having ceased to own a source of income and the rules of assessment which operate on the cessation of a source apply to his share of the partnership income. It has to be said, however, that these strict rules of assessment are frequently not followed and many informal agreements are reached between partners and Inspectors of Taxes in relation to the assessment of such income.

Capital Gains

The principle applied to the division of a partnership's investment income applies equally to capital gains and the possibility of capital gains tax accruing on the disposal by a partnership of a chargeable asset. The essence of the matter is that partnerships do not actually own assets; they are owned by the partners individually. Thus in a firm of four partners who share residual profits and losses equally, a partnership chargeable asset, such as the lease of the firm's offices, is deemed to be owned equally, so that each owns 25 per cent. of the whole. When the asset is disposed of by the partnership, 25 per cent. of the proceeds will belong to each partner and each will have a separate calculation of the capital gain or loss that arises. In particular because of the impact of the capital gains tax indexation allowance which now applies, different partners who have acquired their interests at different times will have a different base cost and therefore a different gain. Each partner's gain will then be aggregated with any personally derived capital gains or losses and will be subject to capital gains tax on the partner in his personal capacity subject to the normal allowances and reliefs.

It will be appreciated that a chargeable event for capital gains tax purposes arises not only when the partnership disposes of a chargeable asset, but when any individual partner disposes of his share of that asset. This may occur when he finally retires from the business (whereupon he effectively disposes of his interest in all the partnership assets) but it may also occur when a partner reduces his share of the ownership of the firm's assets. Thus when the four equal-sharing partners take in another partner, also on equal shares, each of the existing partners disposes of 5 per cent. of the firm's assets, so that after the admission, each partner then owns 20 per cent. of each of the firm's assets.

Strictly speaking, therefore, each partner has made a disposal for capital gains tax purposes, and in the absence of any dispensation, it would be necessary to value the consideration which passed so that a capital gain or loss could be calculated. The general rule for capital gains tax purposes is that where a transaction is between connected persons, then in calculating the capital gain or loss a market valuation is substituted for the actual consideration that passes. In general in the Taxes Acts partners are regarded as connected persons, but not in relation to acquisitions and disposals of partnership assets. In order to avoid the great mass of calculations and valuations that would be required in circumstances where a new partner is admitted to a partnership (or even where the profit sharing ratios are merely altered), the Inland Revenue published a Statement of Practice in January 1975 which laid down acceptable practice with regard to transactions in partnership property between partners.

The Statement itself should be consulted, in conjunction with the capital gains tax legislation, if a full understanding of the position is to be acquired. The general principle, however, is that the Inland Revenue will accept for capital gains tax purposes whatever value is adopted by partners in transactions between the partners in the firm's chargeable assets. Interpreted simply, if a partnership does not revalue in its accounts any chargeable assets, then no capital gains tax implications will arise as partners change their relative profit sharing ratios. If the asset is maintained in the books at cost, then all transactions will take place at cost and no gain or loss for capital gains tax purposes (other than a loss arising through the indexation allowance) will accrue. If, as is often the case, however, a partnership asset is revalued—and this would frequently occur in the case of a freehold or leasehold property or the investment in the firm's service company—the Inland Revenue will accept for capital gains tax purposes upon any subsequent disposal the value placed on the asset by the partners themselves.

Thus if the four partner firm acquired a freehold property for £50,000 and revalued that to £60,000, following which the fifth partner was taken into the firm, each partner would have disposed of 5 per cent. of an asset valued at £60,000, and the disposal proceeds for each would therefore be £3,000. To set against those proceeds, each partner would have 5 per cent. of the original cost of £50,000, namely £2,500, and a capital gain of £500 would have arisen.

Strictly, therefore, where a partnership revalues any of its chargeable assets, a capital gains tax computation is required on every subsequent occasion on which a partner reduces his percentage share in the profits. Where there are a very large number of partners and the percentage change in profit shares is relatively small, the individual Inspector of Taxes may be willing, on an informal basis, to dispense with the need for a strict capital gains tax computation on every change of profit sharing ratios, but will require a calculation of the cumulative gain made by a partner when he finally retires. While this obviously saves a potentially large number of detailed calculations each year, it is likely that small gains made by partners as their profit share reduces slightly would be covered by the annual exemption for capital gains tax purposes so that, had the gain been calculated year by year, the gain might have been largely or wholly covered by the annual exemption from capital gains tax. This short cut system also leads to a loss of indexation relief each time a partner makes a fractional acquisition of a partnership asset.

It should be noted that although the normal statutory provisions with regard to transactions between connected persons do not apply to transactions between partners, where those partners are connected otherwise than merely as partners (*e.g.* as father and son) that treatment will normally not be applied and the Inland Revenue may insist on an arm's length valuation being made in relation to transfers of assets between such connected persons. Moreover, the partners are not protected in relation to acquisitions and disposals between them of non-partnership assets.

Retirement Relief

If a capital gain arises on the retirement of a partner or, indeed, on his reducing his share in the business assets of a partnership, he may be entitled to what is known as retirement relief. Despite the name, however, the relief does not depend on the partner retiring from the business; it is dependent only on his having made the disposal when aged 60 or over or on the earlier retirement from the business for reasons of ill-health. The maximum relief is a deduction from his capital gains of £100,000 and is available if the individual has been a partner for at least 10 years prior to the disposal. For shorter periods of partnership service, the relief is scaled down proportionately.

The relief extends only to business assets—*i.e.* chargeable assets used for the purposes of the trade or profession. Thus it would extend to any gains derived from a disposal of the firm's goodwill or its business premises, but would not cover gains made on non-business investments (including the investment in the firm's service company) made via the partnership.

10 Tax Reserves

Although the income tax liability on the firm's professional earnings takes into account the allowances and reliefs to which each partner is entitled, the assessment is raised in a single sum and the tax is payable by the partnership as distinct from the individual partners. More than that, however, the liability for tax on the firm's professional earnings is a joint and several liability of all the partners; in the extreme, the Inland Revenue have recourse to the salaried partners who are held out by the firm as being full partners, even though the salaried partners' tax liability is not part of the firm's liability based on partnership profits. This means that if any partner should default and be unable to contribute the share of the firm's tax liability which is properly attributable to him, the other partners are liable for his share in addition to their own.

Before entering into a detailed discussion as to the appropriate basis for reserving for tax, we must be clear what exactly is meant by reserving for tax liabilities. What it does *not* mean is the specific setting aside of cash sums (for instance in gilt edged stocks or a building society deposit) so that cash is available to meet the expected demands for tax at the beginning of January and July each year. While the cash outlay at those two dates in the year may be particularly large in relation to the normal monthly outgoings of the firm, it is not appropriate, in our opinion, to earmark cash specifically to meet these liabilities. Rather, these cash outgoings will merely form part of the firm's overall cash flow, a budget of which will have been prepared in order to enable the firm to plan its fixed and working capital requirements (see Chapter 4). Reserving for tax liabilities is fundamentally a book-keeping exercise whereby amounts are charged within the firm's accounts to each partner's current accounts and credited to a tax reserve account in the appropriate partner's name. That exercise of itself, of course, does not generate any cash for the business, but it may preserve cash by ensuring that the partner does not overdraw his after-tax profit. Thus it is appropriate to talk about tax reserves not in terms of how much money is set aside, but on the basis of how much has been charged to partners before determining their net after-tax share of profits which, it is to be hoped, they will in due course be able to withdraw fully in cash.

While, as explained below, there are many other advantages to a firm in having adequate tax reserves, the prospect of one partner defaulting on his liability may encourage the firm to ensure that adequate funds are left within the business by way of such a reserve for taxation to meet the firm's tax liabilities.

What constitutes an adequate reserve for taxation is, of course, a matter of opinion, and practice is very varied between professional firms. In order to illustrate the various methods which are commonly adopted for reserving for tax liabilities, it would be helpful to consider an illustration with the following data:

> The firm of ABC & Co. are looking to reserve for tax at 30 April 1986. Their profits in recent years have been as follows:
>
> | | | £ |
> |--------------------------|------|---------|
> | Year ended 30 April | 1983 | 120,000 |
> | | 1984 | 150,000 |
> | | 1985 | 180,000 |
> | | 1986 | 200,000 |
>
> There have been no discontinuances for tax purposes since 1 May 1980 when Mr C was admitted to the partnership.

The Minimum Reserve

ABC & Co. is by 30 April 1986 firmly established on the preceding year basis of assessment, so that the 1985/86 assessment will be based on the profits of the firm for the year ended 30 April 1984, namely £150,000. A first payment on account for 1985/86 will have been paid on 1 January 1986, with the second instalment being due on 1 July 1986. At the very minimum, therefore, partners must be charged with the actual tax that has been paid away by the firm by 30 April 1986, and this will include the first instalment for 1985/86. However, to refer to such a policy as reserving for taxation is probably a misnomer since in effect the firm is merely accounting for the cash which has actually left the firm and is not charging partners in anticipation of future liabilities. While many firms are happy to provide for tax purely in respect of liabilities on the preceding year basis, on the grounds that by the very nature of the business, tax liabilities are almost inevitably going to be determined on that basis, it would be normal to see provision being made for the liabilities which will have accrued on the preceding year basis in respect of all periods up to the balance sheet date. Thus by April 1986, partners will expect to have been charged with all liabilities on the preceding year basis for 1985/86 and, probably, one-twelfth (*i.e.* to cover the period from 6 April to 30 April 1986) of the liability for 1986/87. If we assume an average rate of tax on the profits of ABC & Co. of 40 per cent. there will on this basis be a gross reserve at 30 April 1986 of £66,000 made up of:

				£
1985/86:	40% × £150,000	=		60,000
1986/87:	40% × 1/12th × £180,000	=		6,000
				£66,000

against which would have been charged the first instalment of 1985/86 already paid.

The Maximum Reserve

More cautious partners would regard the above method of reserving as being inadequate since they might point to the fact that the profits of nearly two years to 30 April 1986 will have been credited to partners' current accounts without an appropriate tax reserve based on those profits having been made. Thus the profits earned in the year to 30 April 1986 will normally come into assessment in 1987/88, and some firms consider that an appropriate reserve for the tax payable for that year should be made at the stage the profits are earned. Such a policy would lead to a tax reserve for ABC & Co. at 30 April 1986 of £212,000 made up as follows:

			£
1985/86:	40% × £150,000	=	60,000
1986/87:	40% × £180,000	=	72,000
1987/88:	40% × £200,000	=	80,000
			£212,000

It can be seen that the maximum provision would have set aside tax reserves of an additional £146,000 compared with those required on a minimum basis. One of the advantages of this method over the minimum provision is that each year partners are charged with tax based on the profits which they have enjoyed for that year. Once the forward cushion of tax reserves has been established for each partner, therefore, there is a logic in the basis inasmuch as the tax charge in any year is related to that year's earnings. By contrast, the minimum reserving method charges partners with tax based on profits earned two years previously, and if the pattern of profits is not smooth over the years, the tax charged in any one year may bear little or no relationship to the profits being earned in that year.

However, this basis of reserving forward for future tax liabilities has two serious shortcomings. Firstly, at 30 April 1986 it is impossible for the partners to do more than make an intelligent guess as to the likely 1987/88 tax liability. At the date of making the reserve they do not know who will be partners in 1987/88. Some partners may have died or retired before the beginning of 1987/88, whereafter they cease to share in the firm's tax liabilities, and new partners may have been admitted. Furthermore, the rates of tax applicable and the partners' personal reliefs and allowances cannot be known so far in advance. The second and perhaps most serious disadvantage of this method, however, is that it is almost prohibitively burdensome on a new partner and inevitably some compromise will need to be made. If, for example, a new partner had been admitted int ABC & Co. at 1 May 1985, strictly he.would have been required to establish out of his share of the firm's profits for the year to 30 April 1986 a tax reserve based on his known or assumed share of the assessments for 1985/86, 1986/87 and 1987/88. Almost inevitably, this reserve would exceed his first year's earnings! Firms which adopt this very conservative method of reserving therefore have to work out their own arrangements for coping with this problem, and this inevitably means that the whole area of reserving for tax becomes moderately complicated and therefore it is likely to be very difficult for the new partner (or, indeed, the established partner) to understand exactly what he is being charged by way of tax reserves, and why.

The Discontinuance Method

It is to be expected that a compromise between these two extremes can be reached, and the compromise which many firms find acceptable and which we recommend is reserving on the basis that the firm is discontinued at the balance sheet date—hence the name the discontinuance method. It should be stressed that it is only an

assumption that the firm will be discontinued at the accounting
date; it is not necessary for that in fact to be a possibility. Indeed,
if there is no change in the composition of the partnership at that
date, then the only discontinuance that would be possible would
be a total cessation of trade by the partnership. However firms for
whom a discontinuance is most unlikely to occur (because, for
example, the firm accounts on a cash basis which the Inland
Revenue will not permit to be adopted for the first three years
after a discontinuance) may still adopt the discontinuance method
of reserving for tax.

Using again the example of ABC & Co., a discontinuance of the
firm at 30 April 1986 would enable the Inspector of Taxes to revise
the assessments for 1984/85 and 1985/86 to tax the actual profits
attributable to those years, while the assessment for 1986/87 would
be on the profits of the 25 day period from 6 April to 30 April 1986
(but assumed in the example below to be equivalent to one
month). Using the discontinuance method, the tax reserve of ABC
& Co. at 30 April 1986 would be made up as follows:

1986/87	Reserve on actual profits		
	40% × 1/12 × £200,000		6,667
1985/86	Reserve on actual profits		
	40% × 11/12 × £200,000	73,333	
	40% × 1/12 × £180,000	6,000	
			79,333
1984/85	Reserve on actual profits		
	40% × 11/12 × £180,000	66,000	
	40% × 1/12 × £150,000	5,000	
		71,000	
	Less paid on preceding year basis*		
	40% × £120,000	48,000	
			23,000
			£109,000

---

* In practice, of course, the first instalment of the 1985/86 liability on the preceding year basis will also have been paid and charged against the tax reserve; the
figures are shown as above to be consistent with the previous examples.

It will be appreciated that the partners have effectively been charged tax on an actual basis—*i.e.* on their earnings for the year. At 30 April 1986 the increment to the tax reserve is based on:

$$1985/86 \quad 11/12 \times £200,000$$
$$1986/87 \quad 1/12 \times £200,000$$

the earnings for the year to April 1986 being £200,000.

It will be seen that arithmetically the total reserve figure falls part way between the minimum and maximum reserves already discussed, being slightly nearer the minimum than the maximum. This will be the normal position if the pattern of profits is of regularly increasing profits year by year. Thus at 30 April 1986 the accounts will carry a reserve on an actual basis for 1985/86 (less the first instalment already paid on 1 January 1986), and a reserve for 1984/85 on the excess of the earnings in that year over the assessment for the year on the preceding year basis. No reserve is required for 1983/84 since, the firm having moved beyond 5 April 1986 without a partnership change being treated as a discontinuance for tax purposes, there are no circumstances in which the Inspector of Taxes can increase the 1983/84 assessment to tax the actual profits attributable to that year. Any reserve on the excess of the earnings attributable to that year over the preceding year basis assessment can therefore now be released back to the partners of 1983/84.

Advantages

There are several advantages of the discontinuance method of reserving for tax liabilities. First—and this is an advantage which should not be underestimated—it is relatively easy for the partners to understand. Most partners will have come from a salaried position in which they will have become used to paying tax under Schedule E on a PAYE basis, which is, of course, an actual basis. The discontinuance method almost always also charges partners on an actual basis, the logic for which can be readily understood.

Secondly, to the extent that the reserves are in excess of the amounts required currently to defray the firm's tax liabilities on the preceding year basis, they make a valuable contribution to the provision of working capital for the business. For example, the £23,000 "excess" tax reserve for 1984/85 will be retained in the business for two years until, say, 30 April 1987, during which time it will have been financing part of the firm's business.

Thirdly, the possibility of a release of excess tax reserves when they no longer need to be retained within the firm against potential tax liabilities gives partners a useful additional distribution from the firm, and enables capital to be built up by the partners relatively painlessly. The regular release (if that proves to be possible) of excess tax reserves also brings home to partners the benefits which they derive from the preceding year basis of assessment. Frequently partners seem not to appreciate how well off they can be from the tax point of view by trading within a partnership and appear always to be looking over their shoulder at the perks and fringe benefits which their neighbours employed by companies appear to be enjoying. If the tax saving enjoyed as a result of rising profits and the preceding year basis of assessment is brought into the equation, the partners are normally seen to be getting a much better deal.

A fourth advantage—and perhaps the most obvious one—is that by setting aside tax on a discontinuance basis, the partners are normally thereby reserving sufficient tax to meet the firm's tax liabilities come what may. Thus although a discontinuance may never be contemplated, it is comforting for the partners to know that if circumstances changed so dramatically that a discontinuance proved to be desirable, there is retained within the firm a reserve large enough to meet the additional tax liabilities that might materialise in that event. Although one could conjecture a pattern of profits which would mean that the firm's tax reserves might not be wholly sufficient to cater for every eventuality (a regularly declining pattern of profits is an example of this) the discontinuance method will set aside sufficient tax to cater for almost all circumstances.

Equity adjustments

The discontinuance method also gives the partners a buffer out of which to make equity adjustments should that prove to be necessary. In order to illustrate this point, the example of ABC & Co. needs to be extended for a further year:

Let us assume that in the year ended 30 April 1987 the firm made profits of £160,000 thereby reversing temporarily the regular upward trend in profit. At that date, the partners will expect to be charged tax on their actual profit for the year, and for their current accounts to be credited with the release of the excess tax reserves held for 1984/85, calculated above at £23,000. However, if the 1986/87 partners are to be charged with tax on only their earnings for the year, the resultant tax reserves will not be adequate to defray tax on the the assessment for 1986/87 on the preceding year basis. The question therefore arises as to the source of tax on the shortfall for 1986/87 of the earnings for the year of £160,000 below the assessment for that year of £180,000. It could, of course, be charged to the 1986/87 partners, but if for example there was a new partner in that year it would be a sorry introduction to partnership life to ask the new partner in his first year to pay tax on more than he has earned in the year. This inequity is particularly reinforced if at the same time as some partners are being asked to pay tax on more than they are earning, other partners (that is the 1984/85 partners) are enjoying the benefit (demonstrated by the release of the excess tax reserve) of paying tax for 1984/85 on amounts that are considerably less than their earnings for that year.

In these circumstances, it would be fair, in our opinion to effect an equity adjustment whereby the tax on the shortfall of earnings for 1986/87 is borne by the 1984/85 partners out of their excess tax reserve before the balance of the reserve is released back to that year's partners. There is logic to such an adjustment. It is the high earnings which were enjoyed by the 1984/85 partners that have given rise to the high assessment for 1986/87, and it is not unreasonable to ask those partners who have enjoyed the high income and a proportionately low assessment to ensure that partners of subsequent years are not disadvantaged as a result. If the composition of the partnership and the profit sharing ratios between 1984/85 and 1986/87 had remained the same, then no inequity would have arisen. However, such a static state is relatively rare in partnership life, and it would be more common, therefore, for some partners to have increased their shares and others to have reduced theirs. The actual adjustment can be effected in varying degrees of sophistication, but the principle will always be that partners who are net gainers will give up part of their gains to ensure that other partners are not net losers. It is not normal for an equity adjustment to be effected where everyone has gained, but some have gained more than others. The preceding year basis of assessment linked with changes in profit sharing rations is almost inevitably going to lead to mixed fortunes amongst the partners but in our opinion an equity adjustment should only be made if some partners are actually paying tax on more than their earnings while other partners are enjoying the reverse position.

It is, of course, possible to effect equity adjustments whatever method is used within the partnership to reserve for tax liabilities. However, the discontinuance method of reserving makes such adjustment easier to effect since there is already retained within the partnership a fund out of which the adjustment can be made.

Accounts Presentation

It is important, in our view, that the annual accounts of the partnership contain a clear statement as to the tax position of each
individual partner. If, for reasons of confidentiality, a detailed
account for each partner is not included within the firm's accounts,
an individual analysis of his tax reserve should be made available
to each partner. In practice, we find few objections to the inclusion
in the firm's accounts of a schedule detailing the balances for each
partner. An illustration of a tax reserve schedule is given in
Appendix 2.4, and it is based on the discontinuance method described in the previous paragraphs and deals with the year to 30
April 1986. A commentary on the schedule may nevertheless be
helpful.

The schedule starts with the reserve for each partner brought
forward at the beginning of the year. This is a gross reserve and
does not take into account payments which will have been made by
the partnership on behalf of the partners for years for which the
assessment has not yet been finalised.

During the year the partnership will have made two principal
payments of tax—the second payment on account for 1984/85 paid
on 1 July 1985 and the first payment on account for 1985/86, made
on 1 January 1986. It is likely that during the course of the year the
assessment for an earlier year—perhaps 1983/84—has been finalised, with a small repayment probably being received from the
Inland Revenue. On the finalisation of the 1983/84 assessment,
agreed amounts can be charged against each partner's reserve for
1983/84, and the amounts previously carried in the column "Payments on account" can now be eliminated and charged to each
partner.

The amount charged or credited to a partner's current account
in respect of taxation will normally comprise three elements.
Firstly there will be the charge based on the profits he has enjoyed
during the year and the best estimate, at the time that the reserves
are calculated, of his allowances and reliefs for the years concerned. Secondly, as the assessment for any year is finalised, there
will be adjustments to take account of the differences between the
reliefs and the allowances assumed when the reserves were originally established and those which ultimately proved to be available to each partner. Hopefully these adjustments will not be too
great, and if there are material adjustments, this will normally
mean that a partner has paid significantly more or less by way of
retirement annuity premiums than was assumed when the reserves
were first established. The third amount to be transferred to the
partners' current accounts is the release of the excess tax reserve

for 1983/84 assuming that the pattern of profits had been such as to enable that release to be made without the need for any amount to be retained by way of an equity adjustment.

Although not illustrated in the Appendix, the tax reserve schedule will also take into account the tax retained for each partner on any payments made by the firm under deduction of tax (*e.g.* annuities to former partners, and any tax suffered at source on the firm's investment income). Tax retained on charges paid will be a credit to each partner's tax reserve; tax suffered by deduction at source on investment income will be a debit. If this treatment is followed, the charges and investment income will be accounted for (correctly) gross in the firm's profit and loss account rather than merely in the net amounts paid or received.

Following all these adjustments, there will be a balance on each partner's tax reserve at the end of the year. This balance should then be explained to the partners in terms of the amounts which are still held (less payments on account) in respect of tax liabilities on the preceding year basis for years of assessment up to the accounting date (in the Appendix £13,600 in aggregate), a small reserve for tax on the profits earned from 6 April to the accounting date (£1,500), and the additional reserve (or excess tax reserve) which could become payable to the Inland Revenue in the event of a discontinuance at the balance sheet date (£11,000 in aggregate). It is the two elements of this additional reserve which are of particular interest to the partners since they represent the amounts which it is hoped can be released back to their current accounts one year and two years subsequently.

A common complaint of partners is that they have little or no idea of their income tax position. We believe that a statement of each partner's tax reserve in this form should go a long way to providing a partner with the information which he deserves to know.

11 Service Companies, Partners' Cars and Partners' Personal Tax Planning

Most partners are naturally alert to the possibility of minimising their tax liabilities. Through professional bodies and normal business contacts, many partners will have occasion to discuss tax planning ideas with their contemporaries in other practices. The danger is that few partners understand the full tax implications of the matters which are regularly discussed; the tax benefits which some boast that they enjoy are frequently grossly exaggerated. For example, it is commonly thought that tax advantage can be gained from a partnership only by means of a partnership cessation for tax purposes and, particularly since the Finance Act 1985, this is obviously not so. Indeed, the best form of tax planning for most professional firms is to ensure that the firm has the most appropriate accounting date, to remain on the preceding year basis of assessment and to attempt to ensure that the profits of the business increase regularly year by year so as to maximise the benefit to be obtained from the preceding year basis of assessment.

Despite enjoying the benefit of being taxed on the preceding year basis partners are always anxious to explore the benefits which they perceive are being enjoyed by friends employed in commerce and industry. Most frequently raised is the question of cars for partners. Another question which is often asked is whether employee-type benefits could be enjoyed by the use of a service company, and the relatively low rates of corporation tax also stimulate more general interest in service companies. These questions are therefore discussed in this chapter.

Service Companies

Service companies were set up by many professional firms in the 1960s and early 1970s when the marginal rate of income tax on earned income was extremely high. In those days, many partners preferred to retain profits within a service company where they might be taxed at 42 per cent. or, at worst, 52 per cent. rather than see those same profits taxed in their own hands at rates up to 83 per cent. Since then there have been two swings in the relative advantage of the rates of tax applied to the income of partners and their service companies.

Firstly, the reduction of the top rate of tax on personal earned income to 60 per cent. accompanied by two reductions each of only 2 per cent. in the rate of corporation tax on small companies (up to 40 per cent. and then to 38 per cent.) swung the advantage away from retaining profits in a company and in favour of taking profits through the partnership. When, in the Finance Act 1984, the long term rate of corporation tax was reduced to 35 per cent. (30 per cent. for small companies) the pendulum again swung in favour of service companies.

Merely comparing the top rate of income tax with rates of corporation tax is, however, potentially misleading. At the risk of stating the obvious, it is worth emphasising that corporation tax only applies to profits which are *retained* in a service company. By contrast, income tax applies to the profits of a partnership irrespective of whether those profits are distributed to the partners or are retained within the partnership to increase its capital base. If, therefore, the partners cannot afford or do not need to retain profits in the business and want the whole of those profits to be distributed to satisfy their income requirements, there will be no question of retaining profits in a service company and therefore the rate of corporation tax is wholly irrelevant. In such circumstances a service company may well not be worth considering.

In terms of retentions to finance the ongoing business, however, a service company clearly has the edge. Consider a partnership in which all the partners are paying income tax on their marginal income at the top rate of 60 per cent. and which has a need to increase its capital base. If the partnership has a service company, the partners have a choice of taking a marginal, say, £10,000 of profit in the partnership or allowing that to remain in the service company. The net amount available to increase the working capital of the business after tax will be as follows:

	Partnership	*Service Company*
	£	£
Marginal income	10,000	10,000
Income tax at 60%	6,000	—
Corporation tax ("small" company rate)	—	2,900
	£4,000	£7,100

It can be seen that a retention through a service company makes available to the partnership business a significantly greater sum than would be available if the profit had been enjoyed in the partnership. In this regard, therefore, service companies enable capital to be accumulated within the business in a relatively painless fashion. However, this is not the end of the story. The £4,000 after-tax income of the partners has suffered all the tax that has to be paid before the partners can enjoy the benefit of the marginal income. In the case of the service company retention, however, further taxation will have to be suffered before the partners can ultimately enjoy the benefit (other than of having it employed within the business) of the £10,000 gross income. This enjoyment will only materialise if the service company pays a dividend, if it is liquidated and a distribution is made to each partner in the liquidation, or if a partner is able to sell his shares in the service company at a figure which reflects the profits retained on his behalf. Assuming that the service company was subject to corporation tax at only 29 per cent. and was able to offset the advance corporation tax paid by the company as a dividend, and that dividend suffered income tax at top rates in the hands of the individual partner, the £10,000 marginal income would ultimately be worth £4,000 in the partner's hands, and his after-tax income would be the same as it would have been had the profits been originally enjoyed through the partnership. If the retention of profits in the service company were to be an interim arrangement to provide finance for the partnership and, for example, on the retirement of a partner he was to enjoy the benefit of retained profits by way of dividends, then the service company would still have performed meanwhile the useful function of providing, relatively efficiently, working capital for the partnership.

It is impracticable to contemplate a service company being liquidated merely to enable partners to extract their share of the retained profits. It is unlikely that a service company would be established with an ultimate liquidation already in mind. By far the most common way in which partners can expect to be recompensed for being required, during their partnership lifetime, to retain profits in a service company is for a retiring partner to be paid net asset value for his shares in the service company when he retires. To the extent that profits have been retained and are therefore reflected in the net asset value of his shares, the retiring partner will realise a capital gain on which capital gains tax, subject to the rules applicable at the date of disposal, would be payable. In the simple example given above, therefore, the £7,100 profits retained (after corporation tax) in the service company would eventually be subject to capital gains tax of (at the most) 30 per cent., namely £2,130, though, of course, exemptions and reliefs may significantly reduce this burden. Taking £2,130 into account, this would still leave £4,970 available to the partner concerned, compared with the £4,000 if the profit had been taken when it arose through the partnership. In the long run (and ignoring interest) the net disposal income of a partner would therefore still be higher through the use of a service company than would otherwise have been the case and the money has been able to be used within the business in the meantime.

There are other factors, however, that should be taken into account before establishing a service company. Firstly, in a partnership where profits are rising regularly and the preceding year basis of assessment applies, the establishment of a service company and the retention of profits in it will increase the amount of profit chargeable to tax and may increase the overall tax paid on the profits of the business. Consider the following example in which the partnership profits are assumed to increase regularly at £20,000 per annum. The partners decide to establish a service company on 1 May 1986 and to retain profits of £10,000 per annum in that company. The position would be as follows:

		Service company established 1.5.86	
		Partnership profits	*Service company profits*
Partnership profits for year ended 30 April:		£	£
1985	£100,000	100,000	—
1986	120,000	120,000	—
1987	140,000	130,000	10,000
1988	160,000	150,000	10,000
1989	180,000	170,000	10,000
1990	200,000	190,000	10,000

The reduction in the profits of the partnership is, of course, reflected in the service company retentions, but those retained profits are subject to corporation tax in the company in the year in which they are earned. The profits on which tax is paid by the partnership or by the partnership and the service company together will therefore be as follows:

		With Service Company	
Tax payable:	*Partnership only*	*Partnership*	*Service Company*
1986/87	£100,000	£100,000	£10,000
1987/88	120,000	120,000	10,000
1988/89	140,000	130,000	10,000
1989/90	160,000	150,000	10,000
	£520,000	£500,000	£40,000

Income tax rate
(a) 60%   @60%   @60%   @29%
Tax payable   £312,000   or   £300,000 plus   £11,600

(b) 50%   @50%   @50%   @29%
Tax payable   £260,000   or   £250,000 plus   £11,600

Partners should be mindful of this possible increase in their tax liabilities particularly in the short term before establishing a service company while the partnership is being taxed on the preceding year basis. The ideal time to start the retention of profits within a service company is when the parent partnership is subject to tax on an actual rather than the preceding year basis.

The Inland Revenue's attitude

The Inland Revenue are perfectly familiar, of course, with the service company concept and, assuming that the company is properly operated, no difficulties should be encountered. However, a service company should not be regarded as a means whereby the profits in the partnership can be adjusted to the required level. The service company's trade is the provision of services to the partnership. Those services will normally be the provision of staff, office accommodation and other overheads, and it is to be expected that any arm's length company would enter into an agreement with the partnership for the provision of those services at a fee which provided the company with a sensible profit level. While, of course, a service company and its parent partnership are not at arm's length, the Inland Revenue will probably not be prepared to see the service charge fluctuating wildly from year to year according to the partners' desire or otherwise for profits in the partnership.

The profit in the service company should therefore either be fixed in absolute terms at a figure which it is expected will increase year by year with inflation or, more probably, the service company will recharge its expenses to the main partnership at a fixed mark-up. That mark-up may be around 5 per cent., but depending on the turnover, such a percentage may give too high a profit retention in the service company. A mark-up in excess of 10 per cent. is unlikely to be acceptable to the Inland Revenue who might attempt to disallow in the partnership some of the fee paid to the service company. A profit uplift which fluctuates from year to year is also unlikely to be acceptable to the Inland Revenue.

Another problem can arise. We have been discussing service company retentions as a means of providing working capital for the business. It may not be possible, however, to lend surplus funds in a service company to the partnership since the Inland Revenue might contend that this constitutes a loan to a participator by a close company. Since the service company will normally be owned by all the partners, it will be a close company for tax purposes, while the partners individually and the partnership collectively will be regarded as "participators" for this purpose. When a close company makes a loan to a participator, it is required to account to the Inland Revenue for advance corporation tax at 29/71sts of the amount of the loan. A loan of £7,100 would therefore require ACT of £2,900 to be paid over to the Inland Revenue. While this ACT can be reclaimed when the loan is repaid, the requirement to account for ACT on the loan effectively negates the advantage of retaining profits in the service company. In practice however, it is likely that much of the capital requirement for the business will fall on the service company, and there may therefore be no need—or indeed opportunity—for the service company to lend its accumulated profits back to the partnership.

Whilst the accumulation of profits within a service company represents an efficient way of providing working capital and may represent efficient tax planning for the current partners, it can give rise to future problems. Incoming partners or the continuing partners are required to purchase from a retiring partner his share of the net asset value of the service company (representing the accumulated profits retained within the service company on his behalf). The arrangements therefore impose a capital burden on incoming partners which, in our opinion, should be avoided as far as possible. This difficulty, therefore indicates the limits to which profits should be retained within a service company. Retentions should never exceed the amount which is genuinely required to provide working capital for the main partnership, and in particular this kind of tax planning should not be allowed to force up unduly the initial capital required of a new partner. The alternative would be to make a modest level of retention within the service company and for all partners to accept that this retention is for the benefit of posterity so that there is no expectation by partners of their being paid out the value of those retentions on retirement.

Disallowable Expenditure

The cost of expenditure which is not allowable for tax purposes can be reduced by incurring such expenses through a service company. The ultimate cost to the partners can, in certain circumstances, be reduced by over 40 per cent. in this way. Consider for example, an item of expenditure of £142 for which it is known that no tax relief will be secured. For that expenditure to be incurred in the partnership where the partners' marginal rate of income tax is 60 per cent. it will be necessary for the firm to earn fees of £355. The same items of expenditure, if incurred via the service company, would require the service company to have income (derived by way of a service charge to the main partnership) of only £200, as shown by the following table:

	Partnership £	Service Company £
Gross income	355	200
Income tax @ 60%	213	—
Corporation tax @ 29%	—	58
Net	£142	£142

Care must be exercised in deciding what expenses can be routed through a service company. If the expenditure is for the personal benefit of the partners as distinct from expenditure which is proper business expenditure but not of a kind which attracts income tax relief, the Inland Revenue may counter the expected benefit by disallowing in the partnership's income tax computation part of the service charge rendered to the partnership by the service company. In this way the disallowance will effectively have been transferred from the company back into the partnership.

Fringe Benefits

Many partners look on a service company as a means of providing them with fringe benefits which are available through a company but are not available to them through the partnership. The benefits most frequently quoted in this context are a company pension scheme and the use of a company car. We need to examine, therefore, whether it is likely that such benefits can be obtained via a service company.

There is naturally, and quite correctly, a great deal of emphasis placed on the pension entitlements of various occupations. While the self-employed person may be bombarded with details of each insurance company's special retirement plan for the self-employed, much publicity is also given to the benefits of a self administered pension plan for companies and in particular for director-controlled private companies. A partner is frequently led to believe, therefore, that much more can be achieved through a company pension scheme than he could secure by paying self-employed pension contributions. While this may be true for older partners who have previously made minimal provision for their own pension, it is by no means always the case that the company director or employee is able to do better on the pension front than his counterpart in the professional partnership. However, many partners believe that if they were to become a director of the firm's service company, these hoped-for pension benefits could be secured by that company. Generally speaking, this hope is misplaced.

Firstly, the pension which can be purchased by a company on behalf of its directors will be related to the expected final salary from that employment and that in turn would be related to the current salary being paid. Thus everything being equal, for large pension benefits to be secured by a service company, it would be necessary for the partners to be paying themselves substantial salaries as directors of the service company. But for reasons which by now should be apparent to the reader, it is likely that from the tax point of view it would be better for the partner to be drawing his remuneration by way of a share of partnership profits rather than as a salary from the service company. Secondly, the Superannuation Funds Office have gone on record as saying that they do not believe that the duties as a director of a service company warrant, for most partners, remuneration at more than a fairly modest level. At the time of their pronouncement, in the late 1970s, they indicated that this rate was only about £500 per annum, and even if this figure were to be lifted to reflect inflation, the amounts would still be extremely modest, thereby supporting only a modest pension contribution. The SFO view means, therefore, that tax relief would not be available to the company for pension premiums which attempted to fund benefits at a higher level. Thus, although the experience of particular partnerships and service companies may not accord with this general principle, it should not be thought that as a general rule large pension benefits can be secured via a service company.

Company Cars

In this chapter we discuss the taxation implications of the provision of cars for partners. The question of whether, and if so, how cars should be provided for partners is dealt with in the next chapter.

In recent years, the Inland Revenue have sought to tax increasingly heavily the benefit enjoyed by many directors and higher paid employees from the use of a company-owned car. The user of an employer-provided car is taxed on the benefit in kind by reference to a scale which varies, broadly, with the size of the car and its age. While the benefit-in-kind charge has increased in recent years at a rate considerably above the general level of inflation, it is commonly believed that the benefit enjoyed by those in receipt of a "company" car is still considerably greater than the tax suffered on the benefit-in-kind charge. (The word company was used in the last sentence since one tends to think of employer-provided cars as "company cars." There is nothing to stop a partnership, of course, from providing such cars for its employees, who will be taxed in exactly the same way as they would be if they were employed by a company.)

However, a partner is not able to enjoy the same benefits if the firm provides him with a car which he uses for both business and private purposes. He is strictly not able to obtain any tax relief against the partnership's profits for the proportion of his total motoring costs which are borne by the firm but which relate to non-business journeys. Thus, if a partner travels for only 30 per cent. of his total annual mileage on the firm's business, he would normally be entitled to obtain tax relief against the firm's profits for only 30 per cent. of his total motoring costs. Strictly, each partner in each firm should satisfy the Inspector of Taxes as to the proportion of his total mileage which is undertaken for business purposes. In practice, it is usually possible to reach agreement with the local Inspector of Taxes on a percentage disallowance of all the partners' total motoring costs charged against the firm's profits, rather than examining individually each partner's record. Whichever method is used to arrive at a disallowance of the motoring costs charged to the firm in respect of a partner's use of his firm's car, it might well represent a less favourable arrangement than would be the position if the scale benefit-in-kind charge appropriate to directors and higher paid employees was applied in respect of each partner's car.

For these reasons, some partners have hoped to secure an advantage by running these cars through the service company and expecting the standard benefit-in-kind charge to be applied to them as directors or employees of the company. However, the Inland Revenue is not always satisfied with this arrangement, arguing that the cars are being provided for the partners as partners in the principal firm rather than as directors of the service company. With the possible exception of the administration partner, this argument is hard to refute. Most professional people are engaged in the firm's business of servicing their clients rather than merely looking after the rather limited business of the service company. In one of a variety of ways, therefore, the Inland Revenue may seek to counter the advantage which it was hoped would be secured and to treat partners as if the cost of the cars was being charged direct to the partnership rather than to the service company.

Partners' Personal Tax Planning

While it would not be appropriate in a book of this nature to dwell for long on this subject, there are one or two general points which should be made. The first is that partners' personal tax planning must be secondary to the overall tax planning of the firm. It would be intolerable for one partner to attempt to block a particular strategy recommended for the partnership as a whole because the end result did not fit in well with his personal tax planning arrangements. The individual partners must plan their personal tax affairs around the outcome of the firm's tax planning, rather than the reverse.

The second point to make is in the nature of a caution. When contemplating personal tax planning the partner must always remember that his taxable income from the partnership is in the main subject to the preceding year basis of assessment. Partners may be aware that they are currently enjoying a highly profitable year within the firm, and may therefore look for ways of mitigating their own tax liabilities. However, the high profits being earned in the current year will probably not come into assessment until a year or may be two years later. Before embarking on tax sheltering arrangements, therefore, partners should pause to check that the tax reliefs will accrue in the fiscal year in which the higher profits will be taxed. The interval between the earning of profits and their being taxed can, of course, work to the advantage of the partner inasmuch as he has a reasonably good idea of his likely tax liabilities for a year or two ahead and this gives him greater opportunity to make plans accordingly.

While the current fiscal climate is unfavourable as far as artificial tax avoidance schemes are concerned, there are a number of tax sheltering schemes which have the blessing or even encouragement of the Government and it is of course open to the individual partner to take advantage of these inducements as he feels personally inclined. First and foremost, the payment of retirement annuity premiums should be mentioned in this context as an essential part of a partner's personal tax planning, but the subject is more fully discussed in Chapter 15. At the time of writing, there is the Business Expansion Relief for the investment of new capital in certain companies. Significant tax reliefs for investment in certain types of industrial buildings are now being phased out, but investment in forestry still has attractions. Various forestry schemes are available, but these normally represent a long term investment.

While it must be up to the individual to look after his personal tax affairs, if he is successful in one way or another, in sheltering his taxable income this may have an impact on the firm by reducing the tax reserves required to be retained for him in the firm's accounts thereby depriving the firm of significant working capital. The question of whether some adjustment is required to compensate for any such differences between partners' circumstances is discussed in Chapter 6. Caution should be exercised before allowing a partner's tax reserves within the firm to be reduced on account of deductions for losses or reliefs arising from non-partnership sources. For example, a farming loss shown by draft accounts may be quite different from the loss figures eventually agreed by an Inspector of Taxes.

12 Profit Sharing

No subject can match profit sharing as a topic to attract the attention of all partners. Yet this, above all other matters, is one where it is quite impossible to lay down detailed rules that are applicable to all or even most firms. Partnerships are a collection of individuals and each firm develops its own personality based upon the interactions of the personalities of the partners. Each firm is therefore unique in that respect and it is for that reason that each firm must work out the method of profit allocation which best suits the attitudes and aspirations of the partners. This chapter gives guidance on the types of approach most commonly adopted, but the variations of detail are almost endless and no account can be comprehensive.

Three Basic Approaches

There are three broad approaches which may be adopted with respect to profit sharing:

(1) equality for all partners;
(2) progression according to seniority; and
(3) sharing according to contribution.

Additionally, in some firms there is *no* recognised approach to the subject. This can result in conflict and tension as partners' efforts become directed to securing their own position in the firm rather than dealing with their clients. This is obviously not in the firm's interest and must be avoided.

Equality for all partners

This approach is usually founded on the belief that it is invidious and even impossible to distinguish between the contribution made to the firm by different partners. How, the argument goes, can one say that a partner who brings in a lot of new work is a greater contributor than one who keeps the firm technically up to date, or who oversees the administration of the firm and ensures, for example, that it has the most appropriate computer system?

Partners who subscribe to this view regard all partners as contributing equally and thus entitled to an equal share. The only exception commonly made is in the case of a new partner. He must be given time to establish himself and his share will probably not equal that of the others for a few years.

Critics of this system argue that in all but the smallest firm it is almost inevitable that there will be perceptible differences in both the contributions and efforts of different partners and that equal shares for unequal effort is no more fair than unequal shares for equal effort.

Progression according to seniority

This is the traditional approach adopted by many established firms over many years. To some extent it is based on the same philosophy as the equal shares approach in that all partners of a given age or age bracket are deemed to be contributing equally. It is justified on the presumption that age and thus experience automatically bring greater responsibility and a greater contribution which should be rewarded with a greater profit share. The critics of this approach question whether just because a partner is older than another this justifies a greater profit share than that other partner.

Sharing according to contribution

The case for and against this approach is reciprocal to those points described above for the other two methods. It is argued that if partners know that their profit-share will be determined, or at least substantially influenced, by their contribution to the firm, in whatever way that may be judged, they will be better motivated than if their share is pre-determined. The critics point to the difficulties of assessing contributions and it has to be admitted that this is not an easy matter to deal with.

Many firms use an allocations committee which usually comprises either a number of senior partners (occasionally the senior partner alone) or else representatives (possibly elected by the partnership as a whole) of each age group so that junior, middle-ranking and senior partners' views can be taken into account. How that allocations committee reaches its decisions is susceptible to some guidance in that contributions of different types (*e.g.* sales, technical or administrative abilities) can be given a particular rating, thus leading to a quantifiable assessment of each partner, but ultimately the decision must be based on the subjective judgement of those responsible. Effort may also be a factor to be taken into account, and that too can only be assessed subjectively as between different partners.

An alternative to the allocations committee is the voting system. Here each partner rates each of his fellow partners (but not himself) in some quantifiable manner, perhaps simply into one of four or five categories of ranking; the results are aggregated and the distribution follows from these combined results. A refinement is for each partner also to rank his fellow partners according to how well he knows them, professionally speaking. The basic ranking can then be weighted according to how well the partner is deemed to be known by his peers. Whatever the system of ranking, however, subjectivity is not avoided but it is at least spread amongst the whole partnership.

One other method of judging contribution is also available: by reference to the financial result attributable to the partner. This requires both fee income and all costs to be allocated by partner. Each partner then takes the resultant share. Such a crude method is not to be recommended, for it is self-evidently unfair to the partner who spends time on the firm's own affairs and thus has less time to generate fee income. The solution is to relate the actual performance against a target. Any improvement over the agreed target will result in a greater profit share. That too is not without difficulty, however, for there will be a natural tendency for partners to seek to agree as low a target for themselves as possible. They may even seek to turn in a performance only slightly ahead of target for fear that if they do very much better, next year's target will automatically be set at a higher and more demanding level. That is clearly not in the firm's interest.

The Composite Approach

While a number of firms adopt one or other of the first two methods described above, few adopt the third method in isolation. Instead, it is common and preferable to use a composite system. The variations are almost endless but a system that recognises each of the arguments detailed above may provide each partner with an identical profit share or "salary" (to that extent meeting the equality point), a second tranche shared according to seniority, and the balance according to contribution. The "salary" element can be set at an appropriate level above that paid to the most senior staff in the firm. Alternatively it can be set at a figure that is thought to equate to what a partner might be able to command elsewhere as an employee of a company and if that route is followed it may automatically deal with the seniority point as well. The manner of dealing with the element reflecting contribution and effort can follow any of the ways already suggested.

The system should be structured so that the proportion of a partner's income that is dependent on his contribution is not excessively high; a quarter or at most a third is probably appropriate in most cases. The system can be refined further to protect individual partners from substantial variations in their shares from year to year by providing that changes (or possibly simply reductions) in the variable element of their share should not exceed a given percentage in any one year. A system on these lines, providing automatically for the possibility that a partner's share might go down, gives the necessary flexibility to deal with those cases where circumstances change and partners' efforts and contributions, whether deliberately or not, also reduce. A system that cannot deal with such changed circumstances will, sooner or later, lead to an unfair division of profits.

A simple example of profits shared on a composite basis such as that described above could be as follows:

The facts

— The firm in question has four partners (A, B, C and D) aged 30, 37, 37 and 48 years respectively;
— the profits available for distribution are £128,000;
— the most senior employees in the firm earn £17,000 per annum.

The allocation

	PARTNERS				
	A	B	C	D	TOTAL
	£	£	£	£	£
• Each partner is credited with a "salary" a little higher than that paid to the senior employees.	20,000	20,000	20,000	20,000	80,000
• With an increment for age.	—	5,000	5,000	7,500	17,500
	20,000	25,000	25,000	27,500	97,500
• Leaving the balance to be divided according to effort and contribution.					

	PARTNERS				
	A £	B £	C £	D £	TOTAL £
• The junior partner is not yet fully established and brings in little new work, but he handles his professional work with excellence and has done a good job in re-organising the firm's accounts department.	5,500				5,500
• Partner B is proving to be a very successful work-getter, is well known in the profession and is building up a reputation as *the* man to consult in a particular specialist area.		10,000			10,000
• Partner C is much more pedestrian. He puts in the effort, but his work rate is slower than any of the others and he brings in little new work; he does, however, deal with the firm's general administration with tact and efficiency and is as effective as any partner in sending out bills quickly and collecting the cash without delay.			5,000		5,000
• The senior partner is regarded by his fellow partners as the person whose opinion they value on both professional and partnership matters. He gets through a great deal of work and brings in as					

	PARTNERS				
	A	B	C	D	TOTAL
	£	£	£	£	£
much new work as Partner B.				10,000	10,000
	£25,500	35,000	30,000	37,500	128,000

- Percentage of share accounted for by discretionary element.

| | A | B | C | D | TOTAL |
| | 21% | 28% | 16% | 27% | 24% |

- Equal sharing would have given each partner.

| | A | B | C | D | TOTAL |
| | £32,000 | 32,000 | 32,000 | 32,000 | 128,000 |

- Automatic progression with age (assuming profits divided pro-rata to the total of "salary" and the age increment assumed above) would have given.

| | A | B | C | D | TOTAL |
| | £26,260 | 32,820 | 32,820 | 36,100 | 128,000 |

This example should not be taken to imply that profit sharing arrangements are to be worked out after the figures are known. It is desirable that they be agreed early in the financial year in question though this need not preclude a later adjustment if exceptional circumstances warrant it. It follows that although the "salary" and the "age increment" will probably need to be defined in money amounts in advance (though they could simply be related proportionately to senior staff salaries), the discretionary element will need to be defined in percentage or unit terms as described in the next section. In the unfortunate event that the discretionary element turns out to be a "loss," the way in which the "salary plus age increment" abates requires careful thought. Generalisations on how to approach that problem are not appropriate as each case must be dealt with on its merits.

Percentages or Units?

The method chosen to divide profits is usually effected either by giving each partner a percentage (or fraction) of the total or by giving him a number of "units" or "points" each of which represents a designated proportion of the profits available for distribution. The advantage of this percentage system is simplicity. The disadvantages are that the percentage share attributable to each partner must be recalculated, perhaps as often as each year, and certainly on the admission or retirement of partners; in doing so it is inevitable that, at least on an admission, some partners' percentages will have to come down. Psychologically, it is usually more difficult to persuade a partner to accept a visible reduction in his percentage than the issue of additional points to a new partner, even though the financial result may be the same. A points system avoids that problem; there is no need, necessarily, to withdraw points from a partner and on admission of a new partner one merely issues new points.

Interest on Capital

If capital is contributed precisely in residual profit sharing ratios there is no purpose in crediting partners with interest on capital. As noted in Chapter 6, however, where capital is contributed disproportionately, equity can be preserved if interest is paid on capital. While the interest represents actually, and for tax purposes, a share of the firm's profits, it is not relevant to the determination of residual profit shares; to take it into account for that purpose would defeat the objective of recompensing partners for having put up more than their fair share of capital. The rate of interest credited should normally be approximately that which the firm pays (or would pay) for external borrowings and it should normally be paid only on fixed capital. If a system of regulated drawings is employed, undrawn profits will, broadly, be in line with profit sharing ratios and no interest need be credited on those balances. If, exceptionally, one or more (but not all) partners choose to withdraw less than their entitlement to enable the firm to meet temporary additional working capital requirements those balances too should attract interest.

New and Retiring Partners

Whatever the manner of dividing profits, a new partner joining the firm will almost always do so on the basis that his profit share will start at the bottom of the range and move up over a period—by whatever criteria the particular firm adopts. But how should a partner be expected to progress in terms of profit share during the course of his career? A composite approach such as that described above will give him an automatic progression for that part of his share attributed to seniority but is there a case of expecting some partners, at the peak of their career, to reach one level of earnings while other more capable partners can be expected to reach a higher level? Similarly should there be a maximum share (or maximum number of points or units if that system is adopted) above which no partner should go? There is no correct or incorrect answer to such questions but if a partner is to perform well and not be distracted by concern as to how much of the cake he will get, he must have a clear idea of how the profits are divided and of how his career, in profit sharing terms, can be expected to progress.

It has to be admitted that sooner or later everybody will pass their peak, professionally speaking. The age at which that happens varies from person to person and views on when this occurs are coloured by the age of the person expressing the view. Nevertheless there is much to be said for recognising that in his later years with the firm a partner may wish to work a little less hard and that in these circumstances some reduction in his share, perhaps a given percentage of his then share at say, age 55 or 60, might be appropriate. If this route is adopted it has the very significant advantage that it ensures an availability of profits for a new partner to be brought in before the senior partner retires. One of the hardest things of all to achieve, yet one of the most essential, is a smooth progression from generation to generation and a mechanism along these lines can undoubtedly help.

Confidence

While partners must be aware of the procedures for profit sharing adopted by the firm, they must recognise that whatever those procedures are, they will contain an element of subjectivity or arbitrariness or both. They must therefore ensure that those of their number charged with the responsibility of deciding how to allocate the profits have the confidence of all of them. To achieve that confidence is an important function of leadership and whatever other partners may be involved in the process the senior and the managing partners will have a crucial role to play.

Cars

An emotive subject, in some ways related to profit sharing, and one which is always of great interest to partners is the question of whether cars should be provided by the firm. If, in the course of his work, the partner is obliged to use a car in order to fulfil his duties there is probably not much doubt that it is sensible for the firm to provide him with a car. For many partners, however, their use of a car for business purposes is probably spasmodic and from a straightforward commercial point of view it might be just as sensible for the partner to use his own car and reclaim from the firm the expense of so doing. But there are other, less obviously commercial pressures for expecting the firm to provide partners with cars. In the first place, a partner's contemporaries in industry and commerce are very likely to be provided by their company with a car as a perk. The partner may feel that in order to be able to demonstrate a comparable status he ought to have a car "on the firm." In any event, the firm may have a reputation to maintain in its local community and may feel that it should provide its partners with cars of reasonable standard rather than see them driving round in old and battered vehicles! Finally, in order to attract staff of appropriate calibre in competition with industry and commerce, the firm may find it has to offer cars to employees. Many partners find it difficult to accept that staff, but not partners, should have cars on the firm. Moreover promotion from staff to partner would then mean having to buy one's own car, hardly an attractive proposition for the new partner.

If, for whatever commercial or personal reasons it is decided that the firm should provide cars, it is important to remember at the outset that the firm is no more than the sum of its partners and that partners will still be bearing the costs themselves. There are, therefore, only two points of substance at issue:

— equity between partners; and
— tax considerations (which have been discussed already in the previous chapter).

The question of how to finance the expenditure is no different from the considerations applicable to other capital items.

Most partners value the freedom of choosing precisely the type of car they require and this is often seen as causing difficulty when a junior partner requires a fast and expensive car whereas some of his colleagues may prefer more sedate and less expensive ones. The solution is to allow each partner a pre-determined annual revenue allowance for his motoring costs. For management accounting purposes, this allowance is treated as an expense of the business and credited to each partner's car account in the firm's books. The allowance can be the same for all partners or can vary according to profit share. The partner's car account is then charged with the annual leasing, depreciation or running costs borne by the firm in respect of that partner's car and it is these actual costs that are, of course, charged in the firm's financial accounts. At the end of the year, any difference on a partner's car account is transferred to him as a prior allocation of profits, either positive or negative. If a partner has chosen an expensive car, the excess of the cost of that over his pre-determined allowance is thus borne directly by him. Conversely, a partner with a cheaper car receives the benefit by way of an additional share of the firm's profit. Equity is thus preserved in the allocation of the gross profits of the firm, and also, broadly, from the tax point of view. All the prior shares of profit flow through to the allocation of the assessment so that a partner who overspends his allowance obtains tax relief for that overspend, while the more frugal partner is taxed in full on his additional profit share. A complication arises if some of the partners' motoring expenses are disallowed, but hopefully such inequity will be small enough to be ignored.

13 The Salaried Partner

The question of whether the status of salaried partner is appropriate and desirable is often asked and impossible to answer definitively. Once again, it depends upon the firm. But it depends also on the actual status accorded to salaried partners within the organisation. In some firms salaried partners are no more than senior employees with their names on the firm's notepaper; they play no part in the running of the business and are excluded from partners' meetings. At the other extreme, there are firms in which salaried partners play a part in most aspects of the firm's business and the main distinction between them and equity partners is the method by which they are paid and taxed. Strictly the tax treatment of partners follows from the role they play in the firm although in practice arrangements agreed with the Inland Revenue do not always accord fully with the theory.

In this chapter we consider the advantages and disadvantages of salaried status and the position of salaried partners in relation to the world at large as well as within the firm.

Advantages and Disadvantages

The principal advantage of a salaried partner status is that it is undoubtedly a useful intermediate stage which can help in the transition from employee to owner. To achieve this, however, his status within the firm must be somewhere between the extremes described above. He should be drawn into the running of the business and the decision making process, even if major matters of policy decision are reserved to the equity partners alone.

It is common for salaried partners to be rewarded partly by a fixed salary and partly by a small profit sharing or bonus element. If such a remuneration package is structured in a manner consistent with the method used by the equity partners for profit sharing, that too will aid the transaction to full equity status. Indeed, there is no reason why the same method should not be used for both types of partner. If the composite approach described in Chapter 12 is followed, this can be applied with equal facility to both salaried and equity partners, perhaps with a smaller discretionary element in the salaried partners' earnings.

The other main advantage of a salaried status is that it gives both the salaried partner and the equity partners an opportunity to assess each other in a way not possible when a person is a pure employee. Each can then decide whether or not progression to equity status is desirable.

Such a process may also encourage a valued senior employee to stay with the firm. If the partners are undecided as to such a person's merits as an equity partner, the employee may well be prepared to stay with the firm as a salaried partner while the partners continue to assess his performance; if, however, he were asked simply to stay on for another year or two as an employee while the partners made up their minds, he might well find that unacceptable and leave the firm.

If progression to equity status does not take place, the question then arises as to whether it is appropriate for the salaried partner to remain in that position permanently or whether it would be better for all concerned if he left the firm. That leads to the main criticism of salaried partner status—that it creates a position which to the world at large is that of a principal but which in reality is that of a second class citizen. To expect a person to remain permanently in that position could be demotivating and in any event to have a body of second class citizens even over a short period could be divisive and not in the best interests of the firm. In our view, it all depends on personalities. We are aware of successful firms which use the salaried partner route as a step towards equity status while at the same time having permanent salaried partners, whereas other, equally successful, firms shun the salaried partner route altogether. It also depends upon the precise status accorded the individual. If salaried partners are drawn into some part of the management of the firm, they are less likely to feel frustrated and demotivated when permanently in that position than if they are treated as no more than senior employees.

As an alternative to a temporary period of salaried partnership, some firms promote staff immediately to equity status, but on a probationary basis for the first few year.

Rights and Obligations

To the world at large and probably also to employees within the firm, salaried partners are indistinguishable from equity partners.

They are responsible for client affairs and can commit the firm professionally in exactly the same way as an equity partner. They are also liable, like equity partners, for the debts of the firm, though they can look to the equity partners for recompense should they be called on to meet those debts. That may not, however, be of much practical value since if they are called on to meet the firm's debts that is presumably because the firm, and hence the equity partners, are in some financial difficulty.

Normally, salaried partners will be taxed as employees and will not enjoy the benefits of the preceding year basis of assessment. Neither will their admission as a salaried partner or retirement from the firm in that capacity, give rise to the need for a continuation notice to be filed with the Inland Revenue in order to avoid the change of partner being treated as a discontinuance for tax purposes (see Chapter 8).

Since salaried partners are, by definition, not proprietors of the firm, it would be unusual and certainly unnecessary for them to be party to the partnership agreement. Instead their rights and obligations and the basis of their remuneration should be set out in a contract of employment which will frequently take the form of a separate letter or agreement between each salaried partner and the firm. Whether or not they should attend some or all partners meetings and what their involvement should be in the management of the business is, as indicated above, up to each firm to decide. Such matters are probably best dealt with informally and not encompassed within a written agreement. This will ensure maximum flexibility and give all parties the opportunity to change the arrangements according to the changing aspirations and capabilities of the salaried partner.

14 The New Partner

An individual contemplating setting up a practice with another is bound to consider the business matters which form the subject of this book. Willingly or not, he and his fellow partners, will find themselves immediately running a business as well as practising a profession. But for many, admission to partnership will be a promotion from the status of senior employee to that of principal and, if the person moves straight into equity partnership, to that of part owner of the business. It can be reasonably presumed, we hope, that the prospective partner will have learned sufficient about the firm and its existing partners to be confident that he or she wishes to go into partnership with them as individuals. But few employees will appreciate just what partnership means from the point of view of the rights and obligations they will then assume as proprietors. The earlier chapters of this book dwelt at some length on those matters and the ways in which firms might seek to resolve, if not avoid, the conflicts inherent in partnership as a business organisation. It can help the new partner immeasurably if a senior partner takes the time to explain to him, on admission, just how their particular firm operates and views such matters. Indeed, if that is not already the practice of the firm, it may pay the prospective partner to take the initiative and seek such a discussion. This should also cover the firm's methods of day to day financial and management control, with which the prospective partner will previously have had only partial acquaintance and even then only from the point of view of an employee. Regrettably, there are still instances where individuals accept partnership only to discover later the extent of some of the obligations they have taken on. While a perusal of each of the chapters in this book will suggest some of the matters that should be considered by the prospective partner, we summarise in this chapter a number on which it would be worthwhile seeking specific information.

But the procedure should not end there. As explained in Chapter 1, we believe that as well as introducing and explaining the workings of the partnership to the new partner, the established partners should devote time to ensuring that the newly admitted partner is fully integrated into the partnership.

Capital

We doubt whether any prospective partner would fail to seek
information about his obligations to contribute capital, but as
Chapter 6 demonstrates, there are a number of aspects to this subject. The following list may help to ensure that all the salient
points are considered before the obligations are taken on by the
new partner.

— The new partner will obviously wish to know how much
  capital he must contribute and over what period. Will he be
  allowed a year or two, possibly longer, to build up capital
  out of earnings or will he be expected to borrow the money
  and contribute the full requirement on day one?

— If he does have to borrow, will he be entitled to a prior
  share of profits to defray the net interest costs?

— What has been the recent history of capital calls on
  partners? While the past may not be a reliable guide to the
  future, it can nevertheless be a helpful indication of the way
  in which the firm's financial affairs have been managed.

— What plans does the firm have for expansion? Will heavy
  expenditure be required for new offices or equipment with
  the likelihood of further capital calls on partners?

— Is the whole of the partner's capital invested in the business
  or is part of it absorbed in gilts or other short-term investments set aside to meet future liabilities? If the latter, this
  may suggest that the firms cash management could be
  improved so that liabilities can be met out of cash flow and
  partners' capital reduced. The prospective partner will not,
  of course, expect to be able to change the rules of the club
  before he becomes a member, but if he is being asked to put
  up capital simply to see part of it invested outside the business he can fairly ask whether this is really necessary.

— What are the arrangements for repayment of capital on
  retirement? This point may be thought academic so far as
  the new partner is concerned, but if retirements by one or
  more senior partners are imminent and repayment of their
  capital would represent a serious drain on the firm's
  resources, that again is a fair point for the new partner to be
  aware of.

— What other sources of capital are used by the firm? Are
  partners expected to provide the whole of the fixed and
  working capital or is proper use made of bank overdrafts?
  Have longer-term sources of finance been considered and
  are leasing or hire purchase used when appropriate?

Profits

This subject too will hardly be overlooked by the prospective partner, but again there is more to it than the simple question of "what will be my profit share?".

— While the initial profit share, and what that represents in net money terms is obviously crucial, the likely progression over subsequent years is arguably even more important. What will determine that progression and what is the mechanism for changing profit shares of partners year by year?

— What profits has the firm generated in recent years (the accounts for the past two or three years should be made available); what does the budget for the ensuing year show? (If there is *no* budget that itself raises questions about the effectiveness of the firm's financial management). What are the existing partners' views about the prospects thereafter?

— Who owns the office premises? This can, of course, have a bearing on capital as well as profits. If the firm owns the offices, the capital required of partners will thereby be increased, as may be the problem of paying out retiring partners. But if the offices are owned by only some of the partners (most usually, the more senior partners) what are the arrangements for charging rent to the firm and what happens when they retire? If the premises are owned by a third party and occupied on a normal arm's length lease, is there a rent review imminent and is this likely to have a material effect on profitability?

— What are the arrangements for drawings? Are profits distributed in full (after tax) within a reasonable period of the end of the financial year?

— What arrangements are in force for such matters as cars and expense allowances?

— What are the obligations to pay retirement annuity premiums? For a new partner, a firm requirement to pay the maximum permitted percentage of his earnings could represent a very onerous commitment.

— In the light of all the above (and the arrangements for the provision of taxation mentioned below) how is his net spendable income in his first year or two as a partner likely to compare with what he took home as a senior employee?

Taxation

Whereas capital and profits are obvious matters of concern to the new partner, taxation is often overlooked until the time comes to set aside reserves in the firm's accounts, or worse, until the tax has to be paid.

— The most immediate matter for the prospective partner to establish is whether there are proper arrangements in force to protect him in his first two years as a partner from having to pay tax assessed on a profit share greater than that which he will actually enjoy. Since, as explained in Chapter 8, the firm's assessment in a given year is based upon profits earned in an earlier year, a new partner coming in at a time when profits have declined could be faced with that onerous situation unless he is protected by an "equity clause" in the partnership agreement (see Chapter 10) or by a similar ad hoc arrangement.

— Of longer-term interest, however, (and also discussed in Chapter 10) is whether proper reserves are made in the accounts to cover the firm's tax liabilities. If the reserves are insufficient, partners may find that they have to meet part of the liabilities out of profits already distributed to them. Excessive reserves by contrast, will result in delayed drawings by partners.

— Does the firm have an appropriate accounting date? The benefits of an accounting date early in the fiscal year have been described in Chapter 8. It is a legitimate point for a prospective partner to raise, for if he finds that the firm draws up its accounts to say 31 December or 31 March he, along with all other partners, will probably be suffering a permanent cash flow disadvantage.

Rights and Duties

Much of what has already been said in this chapter falls under this heading, but a wide range of other matters has to be dealt with by a partnership and these should be covered in a written partnership agreement (see Appendix 1). The prospective partner should therefore ask to see such an agreement and enquire if it is likely to be amended. If there is no agreement he can perhaps legitimately ask whether now might not be an appropriate time to prepare one and whether he could have an opportunity to comment on it.

It should also be clearly established at the outset what day by day duties will fall upon the new partner. Will he simply be responsible for a selection of clients which he alone deals with or will he be expected to work with a more senior partner? If he brings in a new client will he automatically deal with that client thereafter, or does the firm have a procedure for reviewing each new client and assessing which is the most appropriate partner to look after that client's affairs in future? And will the new partner be expected to take responsibility for some aspect of running the firm's affairs?

If it is the custom that, say, general administration is automatically passed to the newest partner, thought might be given as to whether the partner will be able to do the job more effectively with the benefit of some specific training.

Obtaining the Information

Apart from the discussion with a senior partner suggested at the beginning of this chapter, the prospective partner might ask for permission to talk to the firm's accountants. They will be able to advise on the tax implications and offer an interpretation of the firm's accounts. He should talk also to the most junior partner. He is currently in the position to which the prospective partner aspires and will be able to answer questions from recent first hand experience.

15 Provision for Retirement

However young or old are the partners in a professional firm, they should be thinking about making adequate provision for their retirement. For most employed people pension rights build up gradually and almost unnoticed over the years of employment, only giving rise to special consideration when the employee moves from one job to another and seeks to ensure that, as far as possible, his pension rights are preserved. If an employee scheme is a contributory one, the contributions are deducted at source from the monthly salary and therefore the employee never really notices the income foregone.

For a self-employed person, however, the situation is rather the reverse and the years can all too easily pass by without any proper provision having been made for the partner's years of retirement.

There are three principal ways in which a partner can expect to enjoy a flow of income after retirement. The first is by the sale of his goodwill in the business to the continuing partners thereby giving him a capital sum which can be used to buy an annuity. Secondly he may look to the continuing partners to provide him with an income flow by way of a consultancy arrangement or a partnership annuity, and finally, the partner can of course purchase his own pension during his normal working life via the medium of retirement annuity policies. This chapter discusses the advantages and disadvantages of each of these.

Goodwill

It has to be said at the outset that the sale and purchase of goodwill between individual partners is a transaction which occurs increasingly less often these days, and that for good reasons, since it has two main drawbacks. In the first place it requires an incoming partner, or the existing partners, to find a capital sum in order to pay out the retiring partner, and secondly as far as the continuing partners are concerned, it is very tax inefficient inasmuch as they get no tax relief for their payment until they themselves dispose of goodwill, possibly on retirement, and even then the relief is only at capital gains tax rates.

Where payments for goodwill still exist within a firm, the partnership agreement will normally lay down the basis on which the goodwill is to be calculated. This basis will frequently be related to the average level of profits earned in the two or three years prior to the disposal taking place, and will then be expressed as some multiple of those average profits. For example, if the senior partner is retiring and relinquishing 30 per cent. of the profits, he will look to the continuing partners to pay him a capital sum equivalent to 30 per cent. of the sum thus calculated. Typically this would be taken up partly by an incoming partner, and partly by existing partners, each of whom would contribute to that payment in proportion to the share or increased share of the profits they will in future enjoy.

If everyone is happy with this arrangement, then probably no harm is done. Whether the formula represents a reasonable measure of the goodwill of the business is, of course, a separate question. An economist or accountant would probably regard goodwill as being the value of the ability to earn super profits in a particular position. Thus if a solicitor, for example, could earn £25,000 (including pension fund contributions) if employed by a commercial business or another firm of solicitors, the fact that he is able to earn £35,000 per annum as a partner in a particular practice indicates that there is some goodwill attached to the practice. The £10,000 "super profits" then feature in the calculation of the goodwill, (after a deduction has been made for notional interest on his capital) though once again it must be a matter of opinion as to the multiple which should be applied to the super profits to arrive at a valuation of the goodwill.

The receipt of a capital sum for the sale of goodwill will be favourably treated in the hands of the retiring partner. At worst, it will be subject to capital gains tax in full (subject to the annual allowance and to indexation) and nearly 30 per cent. will therefore be lost to the Revenue, but it is likely that retirement relief of up to £100,000 will be available (see Chapter 9).

The paying partners, by contrast, enjoy no immediate tax benefits from the acquisition of goodwill from a retiring partner. They are making an acquisition for capital gains tax purposes, and no tax relief will be afforded in relation to that expenditure until such time as the acquiring partners themselves make disposals of all or part of their goodwill. This could be many years ahead. Even at that stage, relief will only be received at capital gains tax rates, and if the gross gain (before any deduction for the cost of acquiring goodwill from other partners) falls within the limits for retirement relief, effectively no relief will be obtained for any earlier payments made.

Perhaps more significantly the aspiring new partner may be put off altogether from entering the partnership if the capital required of him on his admission—both in the form of a subscription of partnership capital and the purchase of goodwill—is too high. Professional firms are operating today in a highly competitive climate, and they cannot take it for granted that able, young, professionally qualified people will automatically make their way into the practising side of their profession rather than joining a commercial or industrial concern. As we have stressed throughout this book, we believe that professional firms should be seeking to minimise the capital required from partners to run the business, and any obligation on new and existing partners to purchase goodwill from a retiring partner is therefore to be discouraged.

However, such a sentiment is hard to sell to the senior partner who himself paid for goodwill on his being admitted to the partnership many years ago. Transitional arrangements are possible for such a partner as will be demonstrated later, but it is first necessary to consider fully the consultancy or annuity options.

Consultancy Agreements

Tax relief is not available to a partnership for pensions paid to former partners. This is consistent with the general rule that expenses laid out for the personal benefit of the partners rather than for the purposes of the business do not attract tax relief in the business accounts. Thus the remuneration of a partner is an appropriation of the firm's profits rather than an expense of the business; similarly a pension to the same partner after his retirement also may not be treated for tax purposes as an expense of the continuing business. As a result, partners have long sought ways of remunerating a former partner in his retirement in a manner which would attract tax relief for the continuing partners. It was for this reason that the consultancy arrangement was introduced by many partnerships whereby the retired partner was remunerated for giving, after his retirement, more occasional advice to the partnership on matters in which he had considerable experience. In practice, of course, the amount of the consultancy advice and assistance given does not always match the level of remuneration paid, and to this extent the payments could be vulnerable to attack by the Inland Revenue on the grounds that they were not incurred wholly and exclusively in earning the profits of the business. In practice, the Inland Revenue have taken a relaxed view of consultancy payments to former partners, and few queries are ever raised by Inspectors seeking justification of amount paid. It would be necessary, however, for the consultancy fees to be reasonable in relation to the former earnings of the partner whilst he was a member of the partnership.

There are, however, other pitfalls to watch out for. The first of these is a consideration of the National Insurance implications for those who retire before statutory retirement age. This will be linked with the question of whether the consultancy represents a Schedule E employment (*i.e.* a contract of service) or a genuine self-employed consultancy arrangement (*i.e.* a contract for services). Although the position is far from clear-cut, and it is likely that the retired partner will be acting as a consultant simply for his former firm rather than for a variety of businesses (as a full-time consultant probably would be), it would still be normal for the firm to pay consultancy fees to a retired partner without deduction of any tax. This would then be an indication that the consultancy is a position of self-employment, which is the position which will be preferred by both parties. National Insurance implications will flow from this. The consultant will prefer to receive his remuneration gross, and neither the firm nor the former partner will want to bear their respective shares of the Class 1 National Insurance contributions which would be payable in respect of a former partner who retired before the normal retirement age. While of course the benefits from self-employed contributions are considerably less, so are the contributions, and the consultant will probably on these grounds prefer to be regarded as self-employed. As such he will be liable (if he is under the normal retirement age) to Class 2 contributions—the fixed weekly "stamp"—and also a Class 4 contribution depending on the level of his consultancy earnings. There are no contribution requirements for the payer of the consultancy fee.

Self-employment itself can bring the further complication of value added tax ("VAT"). Where the level of taxable outputs of a person engaged in a trade or profession is below a threshold (currently £20,500 per annum) then there is no obligation to register for VAT purposes. If, however, the consultancy fees agreed between the partnership and the retired partner exceed the threshold, it will be necessary for the consultant to register for VAT and to render invoices to the firm inclusive of VAT. The necessity to register for VAT and to complete the regular return required by the authorities is, of course, a burden which many retired partners would be glad to avoid. Moreover, if the employing firm is a partially exempt business, there would be a partial loss of VAT input for the firm.

If the consultant is regarded as self-employed, he may be in a position to enjoy a little further tax planning on his own account. If he has retired from a firm which has an appropriate accounting date (*i.e.* in the period between 6 April and, say, 30 June) and he retires on an accounting date (which would be normal) then he commences business as a consultant at an ideal time in the fiscal year. He may in his retirement and as a consultant to the firm therefore be able to enjoy, to a more modest extent, the benefits of the preceeding year basis of assessment for self-employed people. In addition, his consultancy fees will be regarded as relevant earnings for retirement annuity purposes (discussed more fully later in this chapter) thereby enabling him to make additional retirement annuity premium payments in respect of those earnings if he wishes to build up further his annuity entitlement for when he finally ceases to have any other source of earned income.

Since the consultancy fees are regarded as being a reward for services rendered, the income is treated for tax purposes as being earned income. By contrast, prior to 1974, partnership annuities were treated as unearned income, and consultancy arrangements were thus more common. Since then partnership annuities have, within limits, been treated as earned income. As a result there has been a gradual move away from the, perhaps artificial, consultancy arrangement towards a formalised policy with regard to partnership annuities.

Partnership Annuities

In its simplest form, a partnership annuity is merely a covenant by the continuing partners to pay a stated sum each year to the retired partner or his widow or dependents. Like other covenants, the amounts are paid after the deduction of tax at basic rate. Partnership annuities go beyond this, however. Tax relief is available for the paying partners at higher rates in respect of the gross annuities paid if, broadly, the payments are made under a partnership arrangement to a former partner, or the widow or dependents of a deceased former partner and they are made under a liability incurred for full consideration. There are two significant points here. First, the agreement to pay the annuity must be incorporated in a partnership agreement, and secondly there must have been full consideration. Many a partnership operates as a partnership at will, which means that there is no written partnership agreement signed by all the partners. This does not mean that there is no partnership agreement; merely that the agreement is not recorded formally in writing. Such partnerships will be regulated by a common agreement between the partners and some important agreements may be minuted.

If for no better reason than to avoid a possible dispute with an Inspector of Taxes as to whether an annuity has been granted under a partnership agreement, it must be worthwhile for partnerships who are seeking to grant an annuity to go to the trouble of formalising the agreement which exists between them in the form of a partnership agreement. Any agreed annuity arrangements will then obviously form part of that total agreement. Even if a full partnership agreement is not drawn up, however, at the very least the annuity arrangements should be recorded as a partnership minute.

The other requirement, that the payment should be made under a liability incurred for full consideration is, one would have thought at first sight, more difficult to satisfy. One normally regards consideration for a contract as being of a monetary amount, which would give the annuity the character of a purchased annuity. This is obviously not the intention, and the Inland Revenue accept that the agreement by the retiring partner to retire from the firm represents adequate consideration given by him in exchange for the annuity granted to him by the continuing partners. Within a partnership agreement, therefore, it would be sensible for there to be wording along the following lines: "In consideration for Mr. X agreeing to retire from the partnership on . . . , the continuing partners hereby grant to him an annuity on the following terms."

The nature and extent of the annuity agreed is obviously a matter between the parties and there is a variety of options available. The annuity could be a fixed annual sum payable for a certain number of years or for the life of the former partner. It may also provide for a residual annuity for his widow or dependents in the event of his death after retirement. The period of high inflation experienced in the late 1970s and early 1980s has highlighted the shortcomings of fixed annuities since an amount which might have been considered perfectly adequate in, say, 1975 has since proved to be hopelessly inadequate in the mid 1980s. It is perfectly admissible for the annuity agreement to incorporate provisions for the annuity to be revised upwards to take account of the impact of inflation either by reference to the movement in, for example, the retail prices index or, alternatively, purely at the discretion of the continuing partners. We would not recommend, however, a commitment to full index-linking on the income of a retired partner when such security of income is not available to the continuing partners. If, however, there is no provision in the original agreement for the annuity to be increased and then, subsequently, out of the kindness of their hearts the continuing partners agree that some uplift in the annuity is called for, problems could be encountered. The "full consideration" offered by the retiring partner was in exchange for the original annuity and the now retired partner is not able to give any fresh consideration for an increase in that annuity. In consequence the paying partners would not receive tax relief at higher rates for the additional payments made, the recipient would not be liable to income tax at higher rates on the additional payments and the income would be treated in his hands as unearned income. What is commonly found to be acceptable is for the annuity to be expressed in terms of a share of the profits currently being earned. For example, the senior partner may agree to retire and to enjoy in his retirement 5 per cent. of the current profits of the firm which can be paid by way of an annuity. Care must be taken, however, to ensure that that percentage does not eventually mean that a retired partner is earning as much or more than some of the active partners. For example, if in a four partner firm the senior partner who enjoyed 30 per cent. of the profits immediately prior to his retirement is granted an annuity equal to 10 per cent. of the continuing profits of the firm, initially that percentage might be considered perfectly reasonable. However, if after a few years and a substantial expansion of the practice the number of partners has risen to nine, both the average active partner and the retired partner would enjoy 10 per cent. of the profits, and this could well cause discontent amongst the active partners. A "unit" system of allocating profits would avoid this problem since incoming partners would be allocated additional units thereby devaluing the existing units. If, however, a percentage system is to be retained, equity would be preserved if the retired partner's entitlement was to be expressed as a percentage of the average entitlement of an active partner. Thus, for example, the retired partner might be entitled to 30 per cent. of the average entitlement of an active partner so that when the number of active partners increases the retired partner is entitled by way of an annuity to a smaller percentage of the enlarged cake.

A partnership that goes down the route of annuities (or consultancy agreements) for retired partners must also take care to ensure that the aggregate burden of looking after the retired partners does not become excessive in relation to the rewards being enjoyed by the partners who are still active in the business. Even if the individual annuities/consultancies are not expressed in terms of the profits currently being earned, it may be appropriate to impose an overall limit on the total proportion of the firm's profits which is paid to retired partners. Each firm must consider what it regards as being an acceptable level to be paid to former partners, but there would be a very real danger of the burden of retired partners becoming a disincentive for further effort from the existing partners if the percentage paid away to retired partners exceeded 15 per cent. or 20 per cent. at most.

As indicated above, since the Finance Act 1974 a partnership annuity granted in the circumstances outlined above to a partner who retires from the firm on account of age or ill-health, has within certain limits, been treated as earned income for the annuitant. The limits were originally set by reference to the historical earnings level of the partner in the years prior to his retirement such that, broadly, the annuity was considered to be earned income up to a limit of 50 per cent. of the average of the best three out of the last seven years during which the partner worked virtually full time in the partnership. While at the time this seemed a relatively generous allowance and would have included most annuities, with the passage of time in an inflationary period, partners whose annuities were inflation-proofed in some way found that the annuities then being received exceeded the 50 per cent. limit calculated by reference to unadjusted earnings of many years before. This problem was recognised by the Government and improvements were made in the 1981 and 1982 Finance Acts. Adjustments by reference to the retail prices index are now permitted with the result that virtually all normal partnership annuities will qualify as earned income for the recipient. The importance of these ameliorations was in a sense reduced in 1984 when the abolition of the investment income surcharge rendered the distinction between earned and unearned income of much less importance.

Consultancy Fees and Annuities Compared

It will be seen from the foregoing that the effect of a consultancy arrangement and an annuity is much the same; which then is to be preferred? From the point of view of the paying partners, their principal concern is to obtain tax relief for the payments they are making. While difficulty is not normally experienced over consultancy payments, partners should always be aware of the strict requirement for any payments made by the firm to be laid out "wholly and exclusively" for the purposes of the business. This might well prove to be a point of difficulty if the consultancy payments were to be particularly large. By contrast, tax relief for annuity payments is not dependent on their being "wholly and necessarily" incurred; put another way, there is no presumption that the retired partner has earned any amounts which he receives. The consultancy payment is treated as an expense of the business thereby attracting tax relief in the same form as other expenses such as rent, salaries and so on. Annuities, however, are not an expense of the business but attract tax relief for the partners as a charge on income (see Chapter 9). It will be recalled the charges on income attract tax relief in the year in which they are paid by contrast to consultancy fees which, as expenses of the business, fall to be relieved on the preceding year basis. Tax relief for the paying partners is therefore accelerated by up to two years compared with the relief for a consultancy payment.

In most cases, both consultancy fees and annuities will be treated as earned income for the recipient. Consultancy fees would be treated as relevant earnings for retirement annuity purposes so as to support the payment of further retirement annuity premiums; partnership annuities are not relevant earnings for that purpose. The payment and the receipt of retirement annuities is much more straightforward from the National Insurance and VAT viewpoint. Neither of these impinge on an annuity agreement.

Perhaps the most important distinction is in relation to the widow or dependents of a retired partner. While it might be possible to persuade the Inland Revenue that the consultancy fee was indeed being earned by the retired partner, it would be difficult if not impossible to argue that the continuing partners were relying even in part on the advice proffered by the widow or minor children of a former partner. It would therefore be hard to justify consultancy payments or other payments to the widow or dependents of a former partner and any such payments would be regarded as a voluntary pension to his dependents and would therefore not be allowable for tax purposes. However, as long as the provisions for the widow or dependents of the former partner are written into the original annuity agreement, payments can be made to them in exactly the same way as to the retired partner should he die before the end of the agreed term of his annuity. On these grounds alone, the partner retiring with dependents may well prefer the annuity arrangement.

The Compromise Position

It is possible to obtain the best of both worlds and to combine an annuity with a consultancy agreement. The basic agreement will be for the provision of an annuity for the retiring partner and his dependent, but the annuity will abate to the extent that the retired partner receives from the firm any other kind of remuneration in the form of consultancy fees, directors' fees as a result of his former connections with the partnership, commissions, etc. Thus in the period soon after his retirement as a partner in the firm, during which time the retired partner is indeed more likely to be rendering consultancy services, it would be acceptable for him to be in receipt of a consultancy fee if he would prefer this, with his annuity being reduced *pro tanto*. He might therefore be able to pay additional retirement annuity premiums in respect of that consultancy fee. As time passes and his contribution to the firm diminishes, so can the consultancy fee, leaving the retired partner then purely with an annuity.

Irrespective of the reality of the position, a consultancy fee will be regarded as earnings from work and therefore, if large enough, will prevent the consultant from drawing his State pension once he reaches normal retirement age. The payment of that pension will be deferred until he ceases work or until he reaches the age of 70, if earlier, and there will then be some enhancement of his State pension to take account of its non payment from the normal age. A former partner in receipt of an annuity would not suffer the same deferral in the receipt of his State pension.

Converting Goodwill into Annuity Payments

Whilst there may be agreement with the conclusion that every effort should be made to abolish payment for goodwill within a partnership, in practice it may be very difficult for a partnership just to abolish goodwill "at a stroke." This would impose an unbearable position on a partner who had paid for goodwill on his admission to the partnership particularly if it could be clearly seen that, however it would be evaluated, the goodwill of the business had increased over the working life of the partner concerned. Rather than face the tension that would inevitably develop within the partnership if the younger partners were to seek to abolish goodwill for which the older partner had paid significant sums, a compromise position should be sought. This compromise can be found in the form of partnership annuities.

If a transition is to be made so that a partner no longer looks forward to the receipt of a capital sum on the basis of a sale of his goodwill but rather an annuity in retirement, the sooner that is done the better. This gives a longer period to adjust to the new regime. It is not necessary, however, to make an attempt today to evaluate the goodwill of the firm in, say, 10 years' time, when the current senior partner is due to retire. That in itself would merely lead to more disagreement between the partners. Instead, the goodwill of the firm should be evaluated currently on whatever principles had previously been agreed between the partners.

Each of the existing partners would then share in that value in proportion to the current profit sharing ratios. Let us assume that in the current year the firm makes a pre-tax profit of £200,000 and that on the agreed basis goodwill is valued at £250,000. A 10 per cent. partner is therefore currently entitled to a notional payment of £25,000 for his share of the goodwill. Each partner then decides on the type of annuity which he wants when he is due to retire from the firm at the firm's normal retiring age. The firm should then obtain a quotation of the annuity that could be purchased on the specified terms for the capital sum of £25,000 for an individual in good health at the firm's normal retiring age. The quotation might indicate an annuity at the rate of £6,000 per annum. This figure is then compared with the current profitability of the firm (namely £200,000), whereupon it would be seen that the partner concerned would be entitled on this basis to an annuity at the rate of 3 per cent. of the profits of the firm following his retirement. Alternatively, and preferably, for reasons discussed earlier in this chapter the share of profits should be expressed in terms of a percentage of the share of profits enjoyed by an average active partner. The partnership agreement would then be amended to incorporate the various annuity arrangements agreed for each partner. It would normally also be agreed that any new partners admitted subsequent to that agreement would not be entitled to any annuities from the firm and would not be required to pay for any goodwill acquired. Conversely, of course, neither present not future partners would expect to be paid for any goodwill relinquished on retirement. In this way, the firm has succeeded in abolishing goodwill as between the partners in the continuing business in exchange for the obligation to pay annuities in the future.

Even this compromise arrangement might be hard for an older partner to accept since he may well have already planned what to do with the capital receipt from the sale of his goodwill on retirement. It may be necessary, therefore, to stage the conversion from goodwill payments to annuities, leaving out partners aged over (say) 55 and granting larger annuities to younger partners who will effectively be bearing the cost of the goodwill paid to the senior retiring partners.

The annuity arrangement is much more acceptable to incoming partners even if they realise that they cannot themselves expect any annuity from their successors in the business when they in their turn come to retire. Young professional people seem far more willing to mortgage their futures to a certain extent in order to recognise the "goodwill" of the business which they have inherited for nothing, rather than pay a lump sum on admission to a retiring or even the existing partners. Although the cash flow impact on his net disposable income may be virtually identical (assuming that the lump sum paid for goodwill was borrowed), psychologically most younger partners would prefer the annuity route rather than the purchase of goodwill. From the tax efficiency point of view, of course, the annuity is much more attractive to them.

Capital Gains Tax Implications

As explained (in Chapter 9) as far as capital gains tax is concerned, the Inland Revenue will accept the position which the partners agree between themselves and will not seek to impose an arm's length valuation for goodwill on transactions between partners as long as those partners are not otherwise connected (*e.g.* as father and son). There are two other capital gains tax implications of this. Firstly, the partner who has paid for goodwill which is then abandoned and agreed as between the partners as having no value, might be able to claim a capital loss in respect of the amount which he earlier paid for goodwill on the grounds that the value of the goodwill had become negligible.

If agreed, such a capital loss would be available against any other capital gains which the partner makes in that or a subsequent fiscal year, and it is not restricted to gains resulting from the sale of the goodwill. However, the Inland Revenue may deny such capital gains tax relief until it is irrevocably demonstrated, by his actual retirement, that the partner really has abandoned any right to be paid for goodwill being relinquished. Secondly, there existed a risk that the Revenue would regard the current value of an annuity granted to a retired partner as being the effective proceeds from the sale of the partner's share in the goodwill of the firm. The Inland Revenue have indicated, however, that they will not take this point if the annuity granted is reasonable in relation to the length of service of the partner and his remuneration while a partner.

Retirement Annuity Premiums

The first part of this chapter has been concerned with the income or capital sum which a partner might expect or hope to receive from his fellow partners after retirement. However, unlike many employees who automatically expect their employers to make pension provisions for them via contributory or non-contributory pension schemes, it is becoming less common now for partnerships to have annuity or consultancy arrangements to provide an income flow for former partners in their retirement. Increasingly, partners are expected to make provision for their own pensions, and in our opinion, this trend is a realistic one. In recent years, the limits imposed on the amount on which the self-employed can obtain tax relief for self-employed pension contributions have been considerably relaxed, enabling most partners to make provision during their working lives for an adequate pension for their retirement.

In the 1960s and 1970s, there was a maximum monetary amount for retirement annuity premiums that could qualify for tax relief, and these limits were not generous. From 1980/81 onwards, the limit was expressed as a percentage, generally 17.5 per cent. of net relevant earnings, without monetary limit. The 17.5 per cent. limit is increased to 20 per cent. for those partners who were born before 31 December 1933. There is no distinction in age between male and female partners. The percentage increases above 20 per cent. of net relevant earnings for partners born before 1 January 1916 up to a maximum of 32.5 per cent. for those born in 1907.

The appropriate percentage applies not to a partner's earnings in any year but to his net relevant earnings. In most cases this will mean his share of the Case II profit for the year less his share of the capital allowances deducted in arriving at the figure on which tax is payable. If a partner or his spouse have losses from other trades or professions (*e.g.* farming) these will reduce the net relevant earnings in relation to which retirement annuity premiums can be paid. However, partners should be warned against the desire to pay large pension premiums in a "good" year; it is likely to be the level of profits earned two years previously which dictates the maximum amount of premiums that can be paid and qualify for tax relief.

The general rule is that premiums qualify for relief in the fiscal year of payment. Thus premiums paid in the fiscal year 1986/87 will qualify for relief against the partner's share of the 1986/87 assessment. However, it is also possible for partners to elect for premiums paid in one fiscal year to be treated for all purposes as if they had been paid in the previous fiscal year. Thus a premium paid in 1986/87 may, by election, be treated as having been paid in 1985/86 and will attract tax relief against the partner's share of that year's assessment (subject to the normal limits). An election can be made for a premium to be set back two years if in the intervening year the partner had no relevant earnings. The election needs to be submitted to the Inspector of Taxes by the end of the fiscal year in which payment is made. In recent years, by concession, the Inland Revenue have accepted claims made up to three months after the end of a fiscal year for premiums paid in that year to be set back to the previous year. However, that concession is an unpublished one and it might therefore be dangerous to rely on the acceptance of late elections.

No tax relief is available for premiums paid in excess of the limits discussed; in other words there is no longer any ability, such as used to exist, for excess premiums paid to be carried forward and relieved against the relevant earnings of future years. However the withdrawal of that facility in 1980 was replaced with the ability to carry forward from any fiscal year to any of the next six fiscal years an entitlement to pay premiums for that year which was not taken up. This is referred to as the carrying forward of unused relief. That relief may be obtained in a subsequent year once the maximum premiums for that year have been paid.

Example:

	Relief available £	Premiums paid £	Unused relief brought forward £	Unused relief carried forward £
1983/84	3,500	2,000	—	1,500
1984/85	4,000	4,000	1,500	1,500
1985/86	5,000	6,000	1,500	500

At the end of 1985/86 there is still £500 of unused relief relating back to 1983/84 and that can be used in any year up to and including 1989/90. If the relief has not been used by that year it can be carried forward no further and the entitlement is lost. It should be noted from the above example that the unused relief from 1983/84 is not used up by premiums paid in relation to 1984/85 since the premiums paid are no more than the maximum entitlement for that year based on the year's net relevant earnings.

In view of the tax reliefs available for retirement annuity premiums paid and the fact that the investment income generated within the funds of the insurance companies to which the premiums are paid is tax free, the payment of pension premiums by the self-employed represents a very attractive investment. For a partner receiving tax relief at the highest marginal rate of 60 per cent. a net outlay of £400 will generate tax free income on a gross premium of £1,000. There is, of course, a bewildering variety of policies from which to choose, but it is outside the scope of this book to assess these. Comment can be made, however, on the two broad choices available to a partner. These are between "unit linked" policies and "with profits" policies. Unit linked policies entitle the policyholder to a number of units in a unitised fund of investments. While in recent years most of these funds have performed reasonably well, it should be appreciated that value of the underlying investments, be they in stocks and shares or property, can go down as well as up. The pension which is ultimately derived from the premiums paid will depend, therefore, on the value of the policyholder's units on the date that they are sold in order to purchase the annuity which will provide the pension. If, therefore, the fund is an equity-based fund and the stock market is, at that time, at a low ebb, the value of the pension secured could be considerably less than might have been obtained either sometime earlier or at some subsequent time.

By contrast, the with-profits policy secures annual bonuses dependent on the investment performance of the related fund. Once a bonus has been declared, it cannot be withdrawn and the value of the pension likely to be secured can therefore only go upwards. Inevitably with a more conservative policy, the likelihood of enjoying spectacular growth in one's investment fund is less but the risk of losing out by having to retire at an inopportune time (*i.e.* when investment values are depressed) is eliminated.

Many insurance companies operate a number of funds and policyholders are able to switch between the funds at little or minimal cost. For a policyholder with a unit linked policy, therefore, it is important to watch the market in the year or two prior to the expected date of retirement and to switch out of relatively high-risk investments into, say, a fixed interest fund when it is judged that the market is at a relatively high level. That high unit value can therefore be largely preserved in the final period running up to retirement by avoiding being linked to high-risk funds. In addition, it will probably be wise for a partner to have several different policies and to realise them at various dates.

The other significant factor to enquire about is the return to a widow or dependents in the event of death prior to normal retirement age. Most policies allocate to the policyholder his share of the fund that has accumulated to the date of death. Some policies still only pay out on death a sum equal to the premiums paid plus a compound but low rate of interest. In almost every case, this second alternative will produce a much lower figure than would be obtained from a "return of fund' policy, and in the event of death not long before normal retirement age, the difference in the capital sum available to purchase an annuity could be tens or hundreds of thousands of pounds.

In view of the choice facing the partner, he would be well advised to consult a reputable insurance broker and obtain advice as to the best policies then available. Brokers charge nothing for this service, being remunerated by commissions received from the insurance companies to whom premiums are directed. The partner should be aware that certain companies are non-commission paying, and therefore a broker may be less likely to recommend such policies. As a result, in part, from the absence of the significant cost of paying commission, these non-commission houses often show relatively good investment records, and their own publicity should be carefully compared with the policies offered by commission paying companies which may be recommended by insurance brokers.

Although, not strictly coming within the heading of provision for retirement, all partners should avail themselves of term life cover under S226A Taxes Act 1970. This provides, at modest cost, life cover for the partner and thus a capital sum for his estate in the event of his death before the specified age. The policies are not to be confused with endowment assurance policies; nothing is received from the policies if the partner survives to the specified age. Tax relief is available in full for the premiums paid on approved policies as long as they do not exceed 5 per cent. of the relevant earnings for any fiscal year. Premiums paid, however, count towards the overall 17.5 per cent. (or higher, as appropriate) limit for retirement annuity premiums for each fiscal year, thereby reducing the amount which might otherwise be available to purchase genuine retirement annuities.

16 Mergers and Splits

Mergers

Some firms decide to merge as a cost cutting exercise in the belief that the two business can together be operated on a cost base that is less than that of the two separate firms. While such a philosophy may well be justified, it is our experience that mergers founded primarily on such reasoning are likely to be less successful than those which have a wider business objective, namely the development and retention of a greater flow of business than could be achieved by the firms separately. This may for example occur because of complementary professional skills, or geographical coverage or because the base of clients in the two firms fit well together. But, whatever the reasons, they should be clearly thought out in the minds of partners before the decision, in principle, to merge is accepted. Probably the other single most important factor in the success of any merger is the ability of partners to be open with one another and on their willingness to give as well as take when the finer points of detail have to be faced, either in negotiation before the merger or, with more difficulty, when they arise following the merger. In this chapter we draw attention to some of the points which will require consideration at either the negotiation stage or during the course of implementation. The stage at which each point is dealt with will depend mainly upon the desires of the partners and on their willingness to leave more or less loose ends to be resolved after the merger has taken place.

Partnership Matters

The name of the new firm. This can often prove a stumbling block, particularly if one firm is clearly not dominant in terms of size. If in the evolution of a combined name, one or more constituent parts of the predecessor firm's names have to be dropped and they include the names of families still represented in the business, great care will be required in handling the issue.

Sequence of partners' names. If these are to be alphabetical there is usually no problem. If, however, they represent the seniority, in terms of age or length of service, of partners, care must be taken to merge the two lists of names so that this seniority is respected. This can be important not just in the eyes of the partner concerned, but in his dealings with clients. If they have been accustomed to dealing with a senior partner in one firm, they may find it odd if, in the new firm, the same partner appears to be accorded only a junior status.

Management team. It is important that the correct balance is obtained between finding the best partners for the management jobs in the new firm and ensuring that each of the predecessor firms is fairly represented in the enlarged organisation. While commercial reality may suggest that only the appropriateness of the partner for the job should be taken into account, if one firm feels unduly cut out of the management function, that can lead to loss of morale which itself can have undesirable commercial consequences; a partner lacking morale is unlikely to provide the best service to his clients.

Partnership agreement. It is almost always desirable that a new agreement is drawn up for the new firm. Only rarely will the agreement of one firm prove relevant and suitable to the enlarged organisation.

Financial Matters

Profit shares. The primary decision will usually be the split of profits between the two firms. This may be based on an assessment of past or maintainable earnings and may or may not take account of budgets for the immediately ensuing period. Whatever the basis, however, the historical accounts of the two firms are likely to require some adjustment to ensure that they are drawn up on a materially consistent basis. The most likely area of difference is the treatment of work-in-progress. This can have fundamental consequences for these purposes, as described below, but provided a consistent basis has been used by a firm over a number of years, the inclusion, or not, of work-in-progress in the accounts may not have too material an effect on the trend of earnings. Other matters which may require adjustment include:

— depreciation, either where different rates are employed or where one firm capitalises all expenditure and the other writes everything off as incurred;

— rent, where the property is owned by one firm but leased by the other;
— staff salaries, where the remunerations bands (and bonus payments, if applicable) differ matcrialy so that in the merged firm, the remuneration of one firm's staff will have to be significantly increased;
— pension schemes, where more costly arrangements may have to be entered into by the combined firm to bring the two schemes into line (or even to introduce a scheme where none existed in the past).

It is usually helpful to instruct the firm's accountants to agree on a set of adjusted figures, which can then be used as a basis for negotiation by the principals.

Once the shares of the two constituent firms have been decided, the shares of individual partners must be agreed. It is unlikely that splitting the two parts in accordance with the existing arrangements of each firm will be appropriate. Whatever basis may be in use for assessing profit shares, it is probable that in the enlarged firm this would give rise to anomalies in the shares of individuals in each of the two firms who might on the criteria to be adopted in the future, be thought to command similar shares. This problem will require very careful handling and it is important that it is examined in detail even if not wholly resolved, before the merger is effected.

Capital contributions. Even if both firms contribute fixed capital in proportion to profit shares, some adjustment is likely to be called for to cater for the anomalies referred to in the previous paragraph.

If significant adjustments to capital requirements are called for, these can more easily be dealt with if it is agreed that they should be brought in line over a period of a year or two. Where firms have quite different philosophies—one relying mainly on borrowed capital, and the other on capital contributed by partners, an early agreement on the principles to be followed in future is essential.

Drawings and pension arrangements. These will require to be brought into line. This will not, however, apply to any annuities or pensions paid to partners already retired as these represent a firm commitment by the old firm which must be borne by the new firm. Any difference in the level of costs of those commitments in each firm will have been taken care of in the assessment of profits upon which the basic division of profits will have been negotiated.

Administrative Matters

Premises. The location of the enlarged firm obviously has financial as well as administrative consequences. While a decision on where to house the new firm may well not be possible before the merger is finalised, partners should at least have considered both the cost and organisational implications of a move by one or both firms. Our experience is that the sooner the two firms move into a single office, the more quickly will they integrate into one firm.

Accounting system. Most firms will maintain their financial records on a computer. Early investigation of whether either existing system is capable of expansion to accommodate the enlarged firm is essential. If that proves not to be the case, plans will have to be made to develop a new system. The worst decision, and one that can have disastrous financial consequences, is to leave matters until after the merger and then try putting all the data into one of the existing systems to see whether it can deal with it satisfactorily. If it cannot, the firm can quickly lose the ability to control fees and debtors and with it its overall financial control.

Time recording. Similar considerations apply as to accounting systems. Where both firms record time, agreement will have to be reached on which procedure is to be followed in future. If only one records time, there will undoubtedly be an even greater educational process to be gone through before partners and staff in the other firm accept and understand the system to be employed. If neither firm records time, the occasion of a merger might be an appropriate time to plan for its implementation as part of the control systems for the new firm.

Administrative support. Whereas neither constituent firm might be large enough to justify the employment of a qualified accountant or an administration manager, the proper control of the merged firm might well require additional senior administrative support in either or both of these areas.

Feeing rates and procedures. Both the rates at which fees or commissions are charged and the methods of feeing and debt collecting will need to be reviewed and harmonised.

Staff Matters

Communication. It is natural that during negotiations, partners will be reluctant to tell staff of the possibility of a merger in case this proves unsettling and the negotiations break down. But rumours tend to spread if the negotiations are protracted and it is desirable that some announcement be made to staff as soon as possible. It is better that they should hear official news, even if necessarily incomplete, than that they should hear only rumours which will probably at best be inaccurate and may well exaggerate the implications for staff.

Remuneration and benefits. It is likely that the remuneration levels of one firm will differ, for a given level of staff, from the other. Harmonisation of salaries and benefits is essential and it is inevitable that the lower scales will have to be increased. This will have implications for the assessment of relative profitability.

Contracts of employment. The occasion of merger is often an appropriate time to issue new contracts to all employees. These will, *inter alia,* cover the validity of their service with the predecessor firms so far as pension rights and statutory redundancy rights are concerned.

Integration. Plans must be made for the integration of both relevant professional departments and the administrative and accounts departments of the new firm. It is a good plan so far as the professional departments are concerned, if some staff from the two firms can be switched so that no single department is wholly staffed from one of the firms. This will do much to foster the idea of the new firm and to break down any tendencies for staff to think of themselves primarily as having come from their old firm. Particularly in the support departments, however, it is likely that there will be some surplus staff following the merger. This circumstance must be identified well in advance of implementation and the staff handled sensitively. The problem may be resolved in part by natural wastage or early retirement but if redundancies are inevitable, the way in which these are dealt with will have an important influence on the morale of the remaining staff.

Organisation. In the midst of dealing with the detail of the merger, it is vital that the servicing of existing clients and the gaining of new ones is not impaired. Once the two firms are agreed in principle on the merger it is desirable that the detailed negotiations and arrangements for implementation are delegated to a small number of partners (and, if appropriate, to senior managers), thus leaving a majority of partners free to get on with their normal duties.

Taxation Matters

In general, there is a great danger in partnership matters in allowing the taxation tail to wag the commercial dog. The best advice is normally to allow partners to decide on a course of action which is right from the commercial point of view, and for the taxation implications to be worked out subsequently. In the case of a proposal to merge two professional firms, however, the taxation implications can sometimes become an insuperable stumbling block. The difficulties normally surround the basis on which each firm draws up its annual accounts.

Chapter 2 explained the different bases of accounting commonly adopted by partnerships. When first contemplating a merger, therefore, the two firms will need to establish whether they both account on a similar basis, and if not whether the cost of making the accounting bases compatible is an acceptable one. Let us consider the most difficult combination, namely the possible merger of a cash basis firm with one that accounts on a full earnings basis. Either the one firm will have to abandon its favourable cash basis of accounting and move to a full earnings basis, or the other firm will have to write off its debtors and work-in-progress so as to enable it to account on a cash basis in future. No change is attractive to a partnership; the changes required of either firm in those circumstances are particularly unattractive.

As already explained, a cash basis of accounting is generally the most attractive for partnerships in that capital requirements of such partnerships are usually low. It is to be expected, therefore, that firms already accounting on a cash basis will be reluctant to relinquish those benefits. On the other hand, it would be extremely painful for the partners of a firm accounting on the full earnings basis to move to a cash basis of accounting. Such a move is permitted by the Inland Revenue, but there would be no tax relief afforded to the partners whose capital and current accounts would have to be charged with the writing off of debtors and work-in-progress. Partners in firms where the level of debtors and work-in-progress is at a high level, could well find their capital accounts extinguished or put into deficit if debtors and work-in-progress were to be written off. This would be particularly unattractive to the senior partners who might be expecting to withdraw their capital accounts from the firm within the foreseeable future on their retirement from the business.

It can be seen immediately that the difficulties of reconciling different accounting bases could prove to be an insuperable barrier to overcome, thereby preventing a merger that otherwise had merit. While the problem can sometimes be overcome by conducting the two partnerships in parallel after the merger (discussed below) even this may not prove to be a desirable solution.

The Basis of Assessment

In tax terms, the amalgamation of two firms may not necessarily be regarded by the Inland Revenue as a merger. If, for example, a 20 partner firm took over the practice of a firm with only two partners, it might be difficult to persuade the Inland Revenue that this was a merger rather than a takeover of the smaller firm by the larger one, and a less favourable tax treatment might therefore follow. There are broadly three different ways in which the merger of two firms can be treated from the tax point of view:

— the large firm may be regarded as merely having expanded its business by taking in the partners of the small firm, together with their associated work; or

— the small firm may be treated as coming to an end and the large firm as acquiring a new segment of business represented by the activities of the smaller firm; or

— it may be a genuine merger between firms of roughly similar size.

The tax impact of each of these three outcomes is different and needs to be separately discussed.

Firms of unequal size

It would be common in a partnership for any private clients of an incoming partner to be regarded thereafter as the firm's clients. Thus a young solicitor with a few personal contacts and clients whom he may have been looking after in his spare time, will normally be expected to treat such clients as clients of the firm after he becomes a partner. In these circumstances, it would be most unusual for the Inland Revenue to try to argue that these additional clients of the firm represented anything more than a mere expansion of the partnership's business. It therefore becomes a matter of degree in gauging when the admission of a new partner or partners who introduce a nucleus of work to the firm represents a mere expansion of the larger firm's business or the acquisition of a new segment of business which should be taxed accordingly. The most beneficial tax treatment for the acquiring firm would be for the profits derived from the business acquired from the smaller firm to be treated as an expansion of its business. Consider the following example of a merger between a small and a large firm whose profit profiles are given below. The firms merge with effect from 1 May 1986 and the profits attributable to the business previously conducted by the small firm are taken as

£55,000 and £60,000 for the years ended 30 April 1987 and 1988 respectively:

	Small firm's clients £000s	Large firm's clients £000s	Combined (after merger) £000s
Profits earned in the year ended 30 April			
1985 } Pre-merger {	45	450	—
1986 }	50	500	—
1987 } Post-merger {	55	550	605
1988 }	60	600	660

If the additional profits enjoyed by the enlarged firm are merely treated as an expansion of the large firm's business, they will not come into assessment until 1988/89, and for the first two years after the merger, the assessment on the enlarged firm is based purely on the profits of the large firm earned prior to the merger, as follows:

1986/87	£450,000	(*i.e.* no addition for
1987/88	£500,000	profits of smaller firm)
1988/89	£605,000	(*i.e.* profits of enlarged firm)

The normal cessation rules will apply to the smaller firm. In fact, on such figures it would be more likely, for the Inland Revenue to treat the profits of the small business taken over as a new segment of profits of the enlarged firm and to require that the profits attributable to the segment of business during the first twelve months after the merger be subject to the rules of assessment in the opening years of a new business. The assessment on the enlarged firm for 1986/87 and 1987/88 would thus be an aggregation of profits earned by the two firms but assessed on different bases. The assessment of the profits of the larger firm would continue on the preceding year basis while the post-merger profits of the small firm would be assessed according to the commencement rules, as follows:

	Small firm's clients (Commencement rules) £000s	Large firm's clients (Preceding year basis) £000s	Aggregate assessment on enlarged firm £000s
1986/87	55	450	505
1987/88	55	500	555
1988/89	55	550	605

It will be seen that the assessments for 1986/87 and 1987/88 are significantly increased compared with the position that would have prevailed had the small firm's business been treated merely as an expansion of the large firm's business.

In practice, however, it may be difficult to calculate accurately the profits which truly relate to the clients of the small firm. Particularly where the partnership business represents a series of isolated matters rather than regularly recurring work from the same clients, it may be difficult to identify the source of any new instructions. There may be other difficulties where, for example, both the firms were previously acting for the same client; to which of the predecessor businesses should some new instructions be notionally allocated? In addition, the allocation of overheads between the two segments of the business will inevitably be arbitrary. The profits attributable to that segment and therefore to be subject to the commencement provisions can only therefore be something of an approximation, and it will be necessary to negotiate with the Inspector of Taxes as to what represents a reasonable measure of those profits.

Firms of comparable size

The Inland Revenue's strict view of a merger of firms of equal size is that the business of each is deemed to be discontinued and a new business is regarded as having commenced. This would mean that the rules of assessment on discontinuance would be applied to each of the predecessor firms, while the commencement rules (as distinct from the recommencement rules) would apply to the new firm. It will be appreciated that the application of the discontinuance rules could give rise to an unwelcome increase in the income tax liability of the partners of both firms just at a time when they may already be considering the additional expenses involved in the merger. If both firms are merging from a position of strength rather than weakness, it is likely that the profits of each will have been rising year by year and the income tax penalty from a discontinuance might be so severe as to destroy the concept of the merger. Indeed, if one or both of the firms were accounting on a cash basis and a merger was to mean a discontinuance such that subsequently a full earnings basis would be applied to the new firm, there could be a double blow. Not only would there be additional tax liabilities for the two or three years prior to the merger, but subsequently the advantageous cash basis of accounting would be lost.

Provided, however that neither firm is insignificant in relation to the other the Inland Revenue is prepared to accept that on the occasion of a merger the partners of one firm are admitted to the partnership of the other and vice versa. This is thus a situation where a normal continuation election can be submitted so as to preserve the preceding year basis of assessment for each firm. Although this would appear to imply that two separate firms are continuing, each comprising the partners of both of the predecessor firms, in practice this is not the position and the full integration of the firm which is so desirable from the commercial point of view, can be achieved. Using the figures in the example used earlier (although it is recognised that in that example the level of profits are disparate and therefore true merger treatment might not be possible) the assessments on the merged firm would be as follows:

Year of assessment	Based on profits of year ended 30 April	Small firm £000s	Large firm £000s	Combined £000s
1986/87	1985	45	450	495
1987/88	1986	50	500	550
1988/89	1987	—	—	605

It can be seen that the aggregate profits assessed on the merged firm are intermediate between the best solution (on the expansion of the business argument) and the worst position (on the new segment of business argument). While this answer was peculiar to the pattern of profits illustrated, the continuation treatment for both firms will in fact frequently give the best answer although all three possible solutions should be compared.

It is quite probable, of course, that, prior to the merger, the two firms will not have the same accounting date. That position cannot persist after the merger, and it will be necessary for one or other of the firms—or possibly both if neither has an existing accounting date ending early in the fiscal year—to change their permanent accounting date. Any required changes of accounting date should be effected first after due consideration of all the possibilities, and only when this is done should the date of the merging of the firms, and therefore the assessments, be agreed.

It should be appreciated that although the assessment on the enlarged firm for, say, 1986/87 is based on the profits of the two predecessor firms for the year ended 30 April 1985, the assessment will be divided between the partners of the enlarged firm in the manner in which the profits of that firm are divided in the fiscal year 1986/87. This again illustrate the point that the partners pay tax by reference to profits of an earlier accounting period—even those of a different firm.

Parallel partnerships

In professions where the cash basis or other conventional bases of accounting are commonly encountered, it would not be unusual for two firms in merger talks to find that each has a different basis of accounting. If from every other commercial viewpoint the merger makes sense, it would be a pity for negotiations to fail because neither firm was prepared to face the cost of changing its basis of accounting. In some cases, the answer may well rest in the concept of parallel partnerships. Thus the partners in each of the predecessor firms would become partners in the other firm, but instead of one enlarged firm resulting, the two predecessor firms are continued with each comprising all the partners of both firms. The two firms then continue their separate existence, each preserving its previous basis of accounting. The Inland Revenue will normally accept the parallel partnership arrangements as long as they can be satisfied that the two businesses are separately identifiable and that the arrangements are not being used merely to achieve a tax advantage by, for example, switching profits between the two firms. Thus if the two businesses are separate geographically and there are few common clients, then parallel partnerships may well be viable. Alternatively, the businesses might be within close proximity but deal with totally different types of work such that the clients of each could be readily demonstrated to be independent of the other. In the longer term, parallel partnerships might become burdensome, and therefore costly, to administer and a full merger may eventually be preferable. The possibility of running the two businesses in parallel for a few years following the merger may, however, enable the initial trauma of merging the personnel and the business to be overcome before attention is given to planning for a full merger in the accounting sense.

Splits

The situation where a firm is split into two through the breakaway of one section is a less frequent occurrence than a merger. The administrative and financial problems are usually more obvious than on a merger, for they are mainly governed by an existing partnership agreement or *modus operandi*. Unfortunately, when splits do occur, they can often be acrimonious affairs, with tensions developing as the two parties decide on which of the firm's clients should be regarded as belonging to which of the two successor firms. Normally this is resolved by allowing the firm's clients themselves to choose to which party they intend to remain loyal but all too frequently a split of a partnership generates a considerable amount of bad feeling. So far as tax is concerned it is rarely possible, in such circumstances, to do more than make the best of a bad job.

Almost inevitably, a split of the partnership will mean the discontinuance of the original firm and the commencement of two new firms. Unless the breakaway part of the business is insignificant relative to the continuing part, the continuing partners are likely to find it difficult in the year or two after the split to earn profits that match the assessments based on the profits of accounting periods prior to the split. In such circumstances, it may be better for the continuing partners to allow the resignation of the breakaway partners to be treated as a discontinuance of the existing business. It is then a matter of debate as to whether the commencement rules of assessment apply to both new business (on the grounds that two new trades are commencing) or whether the larger, continuing firm should be subject to the recommencement rules in Finance Act 1985 (on the grounds that a continuation election could have been made on the resignation of the breakaway partners, but it was not beneficial to do so). Without doubt, the breakaway partners will have to commence a new business, and this will be subject to the normal commencement rules rather than the recommencement rules.

It might be thought that agreement could be reached with the Inland Revenue for the profits of the year or two prior to the split to be allocated between the continuing business and the breakaway business, so that both of the new firms could continue on the preceding year basis. The Inland Revenue are most unlikely to accept that treatment. The only circumstances in which such a proposal is likely to be accepted is if there had for the relevant accounting periods prior to the split been separate accounting for each part of the business. If, for example, a single partnership were made up of a separate London and Nottingham activity, and accounts for each profit centre had been consistently prepared, with the Inland Revenue being presented for tax purposes merely with a consolidation of the two profit centres, then it is conceivable that if the partnerships split on a geographical basis, each part might be allowed to be assessed on the preceding year basis in relation to the result disclosed from each profit centre. Circumstances such as these would be extremely rare, and the more common experience would be for the single business to be treated as ceasing and for two new businesses to be commenced following the split. Both of these new businesses should then be subject to the commencement rather than the recommencement rules of assessment.

17 Attracting New Work

This may be a surprising title for a chapter in a book dealing with professional partnerships, yet today, more than ever before, all the professions are facing greater competition, not only from other members of their own profession but from outsiders. The question of getting new work and of retaining and developing existing clients is thus very relevant to the running of a successful professional business. This chapter is not, however, a text on marketing or selling; we are not qualified to write such a work. It seeks merely to identify a number of points that a professional firm might consider as an aid to gaining new work.

The Traditional View

By common consent, the traditional view was that the best way to get new work was by doing a good professional job and thereby being recommended to other potential clients. Such a view is perhaps implicit in the dictum that "a client gained over lunch is likely to be lost over dinner." There is of course, no question but that a high professional standard is a pre-requisite for any professional firm that aspires to success. Without it a firm is not going to retain existing clients and a bad reputation will build up, spread much faster and be remembered much longer than a good one. But is technical excellence enough? We suggest it is not.

The Approach to Practice Development

If a concerted effort is to be made to gain new work a number of threads have to be drawn together.

- the firm must establish what it is already good at;
- in the light of its present position and reputation and the resources, especially human resources, available, it must identify the sectors of the market it wishes to develop;

— it must identify the needs of its prospective clients in those sectors;

— it must identify those features which distinguish the firm most clearly from its competitors;

— it must take steps to ensure that those in the market which it wishes to develop, or those with an influence in that market, become aware of the expertise and reputation of the firm in that field so that when a potential client is considering appointing or changing a professional adviser he is likely to be aware of the firm and at least give it an opportunity to present its case. Naturally the steps that the firm takes must be subject to any ethical constraints imposed by its professional regulatory body;

— it must not neglect its existing clients as a source of new work.

Establishing the Present Position and Identifying the Objectives

A good computerised data base is invaluable when a firm wishes to establish the extent of its presence (normally judged by the number of clients and level of fee income) in a particular sector. Few firms have reliable information on the nature of their work in these terms but even if a sophisticated system is not available or inappropriate to the size of the firm, it is worthwhile conducting periodic manual analyses of fee income to gain a picture of the firm's profile. It is surprising how often such an analysis reveals a different picture form that previously assumed to be the case.

Armed with that information, the firm is in a much better position to review the options open to it; whether to seek to expand on the basis of some existing expertise or, less often to be preferred because of the potential cost and risk of failure, to pursue a completely new market.

Identifying the Client's Needs and the Firm's Distinguishing Features

Apart from the obvious steps of reviewing the firm's existing knowledge of its client's needs and of keeping abreast of the relevant industry by reading the trade press, useful information can be obtained by approaching businesses in the chosen sector. They do not necessarily have to be clients of the firm and in many instances are only too willing to discuss the nature of the problems they face with an impartial but informed practitioner. Attendance at conferences aimed at the sector in question can provide useful opportunities for obtaining this type of information. As a by-product, it may also help the firm to identify and develop its own distinguishing features as compared with its competitors. Hearing from a user why he dislikes this or that firm is a good way of identifying features in one's own firm that may require attention.

Making known the Firm's Name

In all professions, advertising restrictions are in the course of being relaxed or lifted and the option of direct advertising previously unavailable to many firms must now be considered. This is not the place to discuss the methods to be used, but if the procedure outlined above is adopted, it follows that the advertising should be directed at the particular markets the firm is seeking to develop.

But advertising is only one of a number of methods that may, within the ethical constraints, be available for promoting the firm's name. Provided the relevant professional body permits, individual partners or managers can put their name before their target clientele by writing articles in trade journals, giving lectures to appropriate organisations or perhaps writing books on their chosen subject. Booklets and news sheets produced by the firm for the use of its existing clients may also reach non-clients, thus enabling more people to become aware of the firm's name and its expertise. All of these activities can be enhanced by the use of discreet public relations. National, local or trade press, if provided with topical and interesting comment by the firm in a suitable form will frequently publish that comment. It may also be possible to speak on local radio, and if the comments made are relevant and clearly put across, the partner or manager concerned is likely to be asked back.

Lastly there is the matter of personal contact. In spite of the dictum quoted at the beginning of this chapter there is no doubt that when a client is thinking of appointing a professional adviser he will usually think of the person he has met and knows before he thinks of one he has only heard of. How partners get to know people is, of course, up to them individually but they will presumably seek to mix in circles where prospective clients are likely to be found.

But, however good a professional service the firm offers and however effective its methods of projecting its name and image, a great deal can be lost if insufficient attention is paid to the treatment of those who are thereby encouraged actually to contact the firm. If they telephoned, were they treated courteously and efficiently by the switchboard operator and, if necessary, the secretary, before they spoke to the partner? If they called into the offices, did they find the reception area a pleasant environment and were they welcomed and dealt with promptly and efficiently? Failure in any of these areas can result in the favourable impression created by the hard work and expense of projecting the firm's name being dissipated in a few minutes. And it need not be the support staff who do this; nothing can aggravate a visitor more than being kept waiting by the partner or other professional staff when a firm appointment has been made.

Developing Existing Clients

The traditional approach of using recommendations described at the beginning of this chapter must not be over-looked. Given the pre-requisite of a job well done, it will do no harm to let the client know that you are always keen on developing new contacts. These need not be restricted to his own industry. If he is made aware of the firm's expertise in other sectors he will remember this and may well be in a position to mention the firm's name in helpful quarters—perhaps to his bankers or other advisers.

But the existing client may well not be aware of all the services offered by the firm. The director of a company will presumably be aware of the actuary's role in advising the company's pension scheme trustees, but does he know that they may be able to help him with his personal financial planning? If he is not aware of the service he will not use it even if he has a need for it. So existing clients should be made aware of other services available from the firm. Care is required here. To be bombarded indiscriminately with literature about a firm's services, many of which may be of no relevance to the recipient, will do the professional firm no good at all. A partner should get to know his clients and identify their likely needs; the existing adviser is in a privileged position to do this compared with his competitors. Only when the needs have been assessed can appropriate steps be taken to inform the client of the relevant services which the firm can offer.

Organising the Approach

If a systematic approach is to be followed it makes good sense, as with all matters in partnerships, to find a partner willing to take on the responsibility for organising it. His brief should be agreed by the partnership as a whole but he should report direct to the senior or managing partner. And it should be remembered that his task is to organise, not to do. Practice development involves all partners. They can do it more effectively if one of their number has responsibility for the necessary supportive organisation but the best way of getting new work is to find an enthusiastic partner, good at his job who can put across his expertise to others in a way which ensures that they perceive a need for the skills he offers.

By the same token, there can be merit in finding a partner willing to take the lead in organising a firm's efforts directed at a particular industry. This should be a partner who already has some knowledge of, and preferably clients in, the industry concerned. By co-ordinating the firm's efforts in this way, opportunities for business development are less likely to be missed and more effective results can be expected if the firm's activities are concentrated rather than dissipated throughout the partnership.

There is nothing very original and certainly nothing technical in our suggestions. If a more developed approach is required there are publications available and specialist organisations that offer professional expertise in both marketing and selling, and these should be consulted. But it is our experience that most professional men find the transition from being a back room specialist to an effective salesman for the firm to be difficult, if not unpleasant. At least some of the steps we have suggested are within the capability of all partners and if they are acted upon we believe that, over a period, the firm will indeed gain more new work than it would have done without that action.

APPENDIX 1
THE PARTNERSHIP AGREEMENT

1. PREAMBLE
This will list the parties to the agreement who will be all the equity partners but not salaried partners. It will describe the nature of the business and possibly rehearse a brief history of the business up to the date of the agreement.

2. NAME AND PLACE OF BUSINESS
This section is also sometimes used to remind partners of their obligations under Sections 5.1 to 5.7 of the 1985 Business Names Act to display the names of all the partners of the firm at each of its business premises.

3. DURATION
This clause will record the commencement date of the agreement (which may be retrospective) and may stipulate a minimum duration of the partnership. It is not normally appropriate to have a fixed term for the partnership, though it should be recorded (in order to counteract the effect of section 26 Partnership Act 1890) that the partnership is not to be regarded as dissolved in the event of one partner ceasing to be a partner.

4. CAPITAL
This clause deals with the extent of the partnership fixed capital and the manner in which it is to be subscribed in profit sharing ratios, and if this is not the case, it may be appropriate to provide for the payment of interest on capital as one of the prior shares of profit. The rates of interest payable on such capital may be specified in absolute or general terms.

5. GOODWILL
For the avoidance of doubt, it is common to see a reference to the fact that goodwill shall be regarded as having no value as far as transactions between the partners are concerned.

6. DIVISION OF PROFITS AND LOSSES
Profits may be divided between the partners in two or more tranches reflecting, perhaps a basic salary; and residual profit

shares. It should also deal with interest on capital if that is to be paid.

Each partnership will, of course, decide on its own profit-sharing formula. Specific provision should be made as far as the dividing of losses is concerned and it must be made clear whether for sharing purposes, losses are afforded their normal meaning or are struck after the payment of any prior shares.

7. DRAWINGS

It is normal for drawings to be referred to in the partnership agreement merely in terms of "as shall be agreed from time to time between the partners." The partnership should have a formalised drawings policy, however, and there should be a clear understanding between the partners as to their drawing rights.

8. TAXATION RESERVES

The firm's policy should be described in the agreement so the partners know the basis on which they are being charged. Since the preceding year basis of assessment coupled with changes in profit-sharing ratios, instanced in particular by the admission or retirement of partners, can lead to the inequitable distribution of tax liabilities, it is appropriate for the partnership agreement to provide for an adjustment to be made between the tax reserves of different partners in order to rectify inequity which might otherwise occur.

9. PARTNERS' PERSONAL APPOINTMENTS

This clause will record the agreement between the partners covering partners' earnings from appointments as director, consultant, etc., and from writing and lecturing when these flow from a business connection. It would be normal for such earnings to be treated as part of the firm's earnings.

10. MANAGEMENT OF THE BUSINESS

These clauses will record the agreed management structure and the rights of individual partners within that structure. Thus it may be appropriate to detail the functions of, for example, a management committee and any other executive committees, the voting rights of each partner, the matters on which a unanimous decision of the partners is required and those which can be decided on a majority vote of a stated size, etc.

11. ACCOUNTS

The firm's normal accounting date will be specified, together with the obligation to prepare accounts up to that date. The firm's outside accountants may also be nominated.

12. DUTIES OF PARTNERS

This clause will include the normal requirements of partners to devote their time and attention to partnership business and may stipulate that other activities may only be undertaken with the express approval of the other partners. The holiday entitlement of each partner may be specified, together with the normal obligations of partners *vis-à-vis* each other and the outside world — *e.g.* the obligation to be just and faithful towards each other, to discharge their separate debts, etc.

13. RETIREMENT AND DEATH

This clause will specify the circumstances in which a partner may retire, stipulating the notice required to be given in the case of a voluntary retirement. Retirement may be required once a partner reaches a specified age. It will normally be appropriate for retirements to be allowed only at the annual accounting date or, possibly, at the half-year date. The clause will specify the entitlement of a retiring partner or the estate of a deceased partner to the repayment of his capital and current accounts and the release of any tax reserves if and when these are found to be in excess of the partner's known tax liabilities. Frequently the release of these amounts will take place over a specified time scale.

14. ANNUITIES TO RETIRED PARTNERS

Where such annuities are agreed between the partners, they should be specifically referred to within the partnership agreement. This reference will either be to the particular arrangements agreed for individual partners, or will be in general terms relating to all partners retiring in specified circumstances. Where the annuities extend to the widow or dependants of partners and retired partners, these arrangements should also be detailed.

15. PROVISION FOR RETIREMENT, LIFE ASSURANCE AND PERMANENT HEALTH INSURANCE

Some firms require partners to make minimum provision for their own pension by means of retirement annuity premiums, and such requirements should be specified. The agreement might also include an obligation to provide for term assurance to a specified value and, possibly, permanent health and disability insurance.

16. TAX ELECTION AND INDEMNITY

Since a continuation election for tax purposes will frequently be required following the retirement of any partner, it is common for the partners to reserve for themselves the right to require a retiring partner (or his personal representatives in the event of his death) to sign, if requested, a continuation election on the occasion of this retirement. In exchange, the continuing partners would normally grant the retiring partner or his estate an indemnity against any additional tax which might be payable by him or on his behalf as a result of signing the election over and above that which would have been paid in the absence of an election.

17. EXPULSION

This is an unpleasant possibility to envisage, but partners should be realistic and reserve for themselves the right of expulsion in specified circumstances. These will include serious misconduct, a period of long illness, bankruptcy, insanity, etc. In the absence of express power in the partnership agreement to expel a partner, Partnership Act 1890, s. 25 does not permit it.

18. COVENANTS IN RESTRAINT OF TRADE

This clause would impose limits on a retiring or expelled partner from practising in competition with former partners within, say, a certain radius of the existing offices and for a certain period of years. These limits must be reasonable or it may be found that in practice they are unenforceable.

19. ARBITRATOR

It would be normal to provide for arbitration in the event of an irreconcilable disagreement between partners. The arbitrator would normally be a prominent personality of the profession concerned (*e.g.* the President of the Law Society); some professions require the arbitrator to be a member of that profession (*e.g.* an arbitrator between members of the Stock Exchange has to be such a member himself).

20. NOTICES ETC

These will be the familiar clauses concerning the delivery of notices by post, etc.

APPENDIX 2
THE FIRM'S ACCOUNTS

CONTENTS

Introduction

This appendix illustrates our suggested format for presentation of the principal pages of a partnership's annual accounts. Whilst there are alternative formats available, and any firm may wish to provide greater or lesser detail by way of supporting analyses in the accounts, the attached examples are designed to provide the main information in a clear and concise way.

The notes dealing with partners' funds in Appendices 2.3 and 2.4 link movements on partners' accounts and tax reserves to the results as disclosed by the Profit and Loss accounts in Appendix 2.1 and to the overall movements on the balance sheet in Appendix 2.2.

The fixed asset note enables the reader to see how movements in the balances for fixed assets shown in the balance sheet are linked to purchases and disposals of fixed assets and the depreciation charge in the profit and loss account.

Finally, the source and application of funds statement illustrated in Appendix 2.6 shows how the cash generated from the profits of the firm and from other sources has been applied and how any movement in retained working capital is made up. This statement can help in analysing why availability of cash for distribution to partners does not always follow from making profits! The notes in

Appendix 2.7 explain the way in which the figures in the source and application of funds statement are derived from the information provided in Appendices 2.1 to 2.5 inclusive.

Appendix 2.1

Partnership Profit and Loss Account for the Year Ending 30 April 1986

		1986 £		1985 £
INCOME				
Fees rendered		287,017		253,944
Increase (decrease) in work in progress		14,400		6,609
		301,417		260,553
*Sundry Income		5,872		6,873
		307,289		267,426
EXPENDITURE				
*Employee costs	146,123		120,103	
*Establishment costs	48,661		39,720	
*Office expenses	46,503		42,352	
*Financial expenses	12,950		11,760	
*Other costs	5,585	259,822	4,324	218,259
NET PRACTISING PROFIT		47,467		49,167
Interest received less paid		9,577		6,346
PROFIT FOR THE YEAR FOR PARTNERS		£57,044		£55,513

* Supported by subsidiary analyses as appropriate

Appendix 2.2

Partnership Balance Sheet 30 April 1986

		1986 £		1985 £
PARTNERS' FUNDS AND TAX RESERVES				
Capital accounts (Appendix 2.3)		40,000		30,000
Current accounts (Appendix 2.3)		79,893		75,534
		119,893		105,534
Taxation reserves (Appendix 2.4)		26,100		18,921
FUNDS EMPLOYED		£145,993		£124,455
EMPLOYMENT OF FUNDS				
FIXED ASSETS (Appendix 2.5)		16,463		4,912
CURRENT ASSETS				
Work-in-Progress	201,919		187,519	
Client debtors	103,834		103,726	
Disbursements	21,503		18,611	
Other debtors	4,310		29,590	
Bank balances and cash	49,095		220	
	380,661		339,666	
CURRENT LIABILITIES (excluding taxation)				
Creditors and accruals	121,875		97,268	
Bank overdraft	129,256		122,855	
	251,131		220,123	
NET CURRENT ASSETS		129,530		119,543
		£145,993		£124,455

Appendix 2.2—cont.

Partnership Balance Sheet 30 April 1986

	1986 £	1985 £
LIABILITIES TO CLIENTS	£297,759	£255,346
represented by CLIENTS' MONEY (HELD AT BANKS)	£297,759	£255,346

Appendix 2.3

Partners' Funds for the Year Ending 30 April 1986

	A £	B £	C £	TOTAL £
CAPITAL ACCOUNTS				
Balance 1 May 1985	16,667	10,000	3,333	30,000
Capital introduced	—	5,000	6,667	11,667
Capital repaid	(1,667)	—	—	(1,667)
Balance 30 April 1986	£15,000	£15,000	£10,000	£40,000
CURRENT ACCOUNTS				
Balance 1 May 1985	32,945	23,862	18,727	75,534
Profit for the year	23,673	18,249	15,122	57,044
Taxation charge for the year	(10,653)	(8,212)	(6,805)	(25,670)
Release of taxation reserves no longer required	2,100	1,750	1,200	5,050
Other tax adjustments	181	45	(23)	203
Drawings	(11,536)	(10,139)	(10,593)	(32,268)
Balance 30 April 1986	£36,710	£25,555	£17,628	£79,893

Appendix 2.4

Partnership Tax Reserves, 30 April 1986

	Partners A	Partners B	Partners C	Sub-total	Payments on account	TOTAL
Balance 1 May 1985	18,732	16,480	10,609	45,821	(26,900)	18,921
Repayments/(payments) during year						
1983/84					1,762	1,762
1984/85					(7,000)	(7,000)
1985/86					(8,000)	(8,000)
Allocation of payment for 1983/84	(8,619)	(5,924)	(3,867)	(18,410)	18,410	—
Charge for year:						
Based on profits for year	10,653	8,212	6,805	25,670	—	25,670
Prior year adjustments	(181)	(45)	23	(203)	—	(203)
Release of excess reserve for 1983/4	(2,100)	(1,750)	(1,200)	(5,050)	—	(5,050)
Balance at 30 April 1986	£18,485	£16,973	£12,370	£47,828	£(21,728)	£26,100
Representing						
Income tax inevitably payable on the preceding year basis for						
1984/85	2,485	5,673	4,670	12,828	(13,728)	(900)
1985/86	10,400	6,900	5,200	22,500	(8,000)	14,500
Reserve for income tax on actual profits of 25 days from 6 to 30 April 1986	700	500	300	1,500	—	1,500
Additional reserve against the possibility of a discontinuance of the firm at 30 April 1986						
1984/85	2,100	1,800	950	4,850	—	4,850
1985/86	2,800	2,100	1,250	6,150	—	6,150
	£18,485	£16,973	£12,370	£47,828	£(21,728)	£26,100

Appendix 2.5

Partnership Accounts: Fixed Asset Analysis

FIXED ASSETS

	Motor vehicles £	Fixtures & fittings £	TOTAL £
COST			
Cost at 1 May 1985	7,518	6,687	14,205
Additions during year	12,386	5,704	18,090
Disposals during year	—	(1,918)	(1,918)
Cost at 30 April 1986	19,904	10,473	30,377
DEPRECIATION			
Depreciation at 1st May 1985	1,879	7,414	9,293
On disposals during year	—	(1,402)	(1,402)
Charge for year	4,976	1,047	6,023
Depreciation at 30 April 1986	6,855	7,059	13,914
NET BOOK VALUE at 30 April 1986	£13,049	£3,414	£16,463

DISPOSALS (Note)	
Sale proceeds	110
Net book value of disposals	516
Profit (loss) on disposal	£(406)

Note: Information on disposals would not normally be included in the accounts; it is included here solely to illustrate the preparation of part of the funds statement (Appendix 2.6).

Appendix 2.6

Partnership Statement of Source and Application of Funds

SOURCE OF FUNDS		1986 £		1985 £
Profit before tax		57,044		55,513
Items not involving the movement of funds				
Depreciation	6,023		2,474	
Loss (profit) on disposal of fixed assets	406		(1,337)	
		6,429		1,137
FUNDS GENERATED FROM OPERATIONS		63,473		56,650
OTHER SOURCES				
Proceeds of sales of fixed assets	110		1,337	
Taxation repaid	1,762		562	
		1,872		1,899
		65,345		58,549
PARTNERS' FUNDS INTRODUCED (WITHDRAWN)				
Capital introduced	11,667		—	
Capital repaid	(1,667)		—	
Drawings	(32,268)		(39,718)	
		(22,268)		(39,718)
		43,077		18,831
APPLICATION OF FUNDS				
Purchases of fixed assets	18,090		7,942	
Taxation paid	15,000		16,500	
		(33,090)		(24,442)
INCREASE IN WORKING CAPITAL		£9,987		£(5,611)

Appendix 2.6—cont.

Partnership Statement of Source and Application of Funds

	1986 £	1985 £
REPRESENTED BY:		
Increase in work-in-progress	14,400	6,600
Increase in client debtors	108	—
Increase in disbursements outstanding	2,892	1,964
(Decrease) increase in sundry debtors	(25,280)	4,338
Increase (decrease) in cash and bank balances	48,875	(11,210)
(Increase) decrease in creditors	(24,607)	8,742
(Increase) in overdrafts	(6,401)	(16,045)
	£9,987	£(5,611)

Appendix 2.7

Preparation of the Funds Statement

The purpose of the statement of the source and application of funds ("funds statement") is to demonstrate the sources from which the firm's funds have been derived during the period to which the accounts relate, the way in which they have been applied, and the resulting changes in the working capital of the firm. The statement is a useful summary of the changes to the state of the firm's finances over the year under review.

The following notes are designed to assist in the preparation of the funds statement from the accounts.

It is important to appreciate that the funds statement is an analysis of the movements between the opening and the closing balance sheets of the firm. Part of that movement is represented by the profit or loss in the year and it is therefore logical to start with that figure, particularly as profits earned will normally be the major source of funds to the business. The figure will need to be adjusted for any charges made or credits received in arriving at the profits but which do not involve the movement of funds. Depreciation is the most usual example of such charges since it represents an allocation to the profit and loss account of a proportion of the cost of assets rather than a specific cash outflow such as expenditure on fixed assets acquired. Other examples of items not involving funds movements are unrealised exchange profits and losses and profits or losses on assets sold, since the actual proceeds on asset disposals are dealt with as a separate item in the funds statement.

The profit so adjusted represents the funds generated from operations; to this must be added funds from other sources. Apart from transactions involving partners, which are probably best dealt with separately, typical examples are new loans introduced to the business and proceeds from disposals of assets. Such transactions are normally readily identified from a review of balance sheet movements. It is important to reconcile the figures in the balance sheet with the profit or loss shown in the profit and loss account and the actual proceeds of disposal. Using the figures in Appendices 2.5 and 2.6 the reconciliation would be as follows:

	£
Cost of fixed assets disposed of	1,918
Depreciation to date of disposal	(1,402)
Net book value at disposal	516
Loss on disposal	(406)
Proceeds from disposal as shown in the funds statement	£110

Transactions involving partners may either be dealt with separately as a source of funds, (*e.g.* capital introduced,) or an application of funds, (*e.g.* drawings,) or be dealt with together as illustrated in Appendix 2.6. The approach selected should be that which is found to be most helpful to the partners.

The profits which form the starting point for the funds statement are taken before taxation so that the actual tax paid rather than the movement in tax reserves can be taken into account. To ensure that the figure for tax paid is correct a reconciliation of the movements should be carried out as follows (using the figures in Appendices 2.4 and 2.6):

Provision for taxation brought forward	18,921
Taxation charge for the year (net of releases and prior year adjustments)	20,417
	39,338
Provision for taxation carried forward	(26,100)
	£13,238
Taxation paid	15,000
Taxation refunded	(1,762)
	£13,238

The tax paid figure will be included as an application of funds together with expenditure on fixed assets and any other similar items, *e.g.* repayment of loans. It is important to distinguish in the funds statement between loans which provide funding for specified periods and overdraft funding which is a part of working capital.

At this stage it is useful to consider whether there are any other transactions which may have occurred which require special recognition. These will usually be apparent as being exceptional. One example might be the acquisition of another business in the year. Such a transaction will require special representation which will depend on whether or not specified assets and liabilities are acquired. The treatment and presentation will depend on the circumstances of each such arrangement.

The aggregation of the items described above will give the net movement of funds in the year. This is then analysed as the net movement of each of the items which constitute working capital, namely work-in-progress, debtors, cash, creditors (other than taxation), and overdraft finance, thereby proving the arithmetical accuracy of the statement.

APPENDIX 3
THE CASH FLOW FORECAST

CONTENTS

Introduction

The first step in compiling a 12 month cash flow forecast is the preparation of a budgeted profit and loss account for the firm covering the relevant period (see Chapter 4). Once this is available and has been agreed the timings of both income and expenses can be assessed for inclusion in the cash forecast. All income and expense items which are subject to VAT will need to be grossed up to include the amounts of VAT which will additionally be collected and paid over. The net of these amounts for each VAT period will form the basis of the figure for VAT payment or receipt to be included in the forecast.

Capital expenditure and any cash realised from disposals of assets will also need to be estimated, together with its timing. These amounts will influence the depreciation charge in the Profit and Loss account. Accordingly the movements on fixed assets should be scheduled, the depreciation computed and any adjustment to the forecast Profit and Loss account made (see Appendix 3.4).

The cash flow forecast (Appendix 3.2) can now be prepared taking into account estimates of partners' drawings and taxation payments. The forecast will provide figures for closing cash and loan balances together with an indication of when the lowest and highest cash or overdraft balances will occur. It should be borne in mind that cash flows within each month may be such that the month end balances do not represent the true maximum and minimum balances. A review of the forecast may indicate that a reassessment is required, for example if the indicated overdraft is greater than the facility that the bank currently provides.

However, before a cash flow forecast is accepted as being correct it is wise to prepare a forecast closing balance sheet (Appendix 3.5). This will not ony prove the arithmetical accuracy of the exercise but may also reveal figures that appear anomolous by reference to current experience; investigation of any such anomolies may then reveal that unrealistic assumptions have been made about the timing of cash flows. Notes on the preparation of a forecast balance sheet appear in Appendix 3.7.

For convenience the attached appendices are prepared so as to link to the partnership accounts included in Appendix 2. Accordingly, the opening balance sheet is that included in Appendix 2.2 and the forecast profit and loss account is one that might reasonably follow from the actual profit and loss account in Appendix 2.1

Appendix 3.1

Partnership, Cash Flow Forecast, for the Year Ending 30 April 1987

£'000's

	MAY	JUNE	JULY	AUG	SEPT	OCT	NOV	DEC	JAN	FEB	MAR	APR	TOTAL
Receipts													
Fees/Commission (inc VAT)	41	36	23	18	24	37	29	30	23	29	29	35	354
Sundry		3			3			4			5		15
TOTAL INCOME	41	39	23	18	27	37	29	34	23	29	34	35	369
Payments													
Salaries (net)	8	8	8	9	9	10	10	11	10	10	10	11	114
PAYE/NIC	2	2	2	2	3	3	4	4	4	4	4	4	38
VAT		11			7			7			8		33
Rent and Rates		15			10			15			10		50
Other Expenses	5	5	5	5	6	5	5	8	5	6	6	6	67
Capital Expenditure				5	15	3							23
Partners' Drawings —monthly	2	2	2	2	2	2	2	2	2	2	2	2	24
—special	4		3		4			4			4		19
Income tax			9				(1)		10				18
TOTAL PAYMENTS	21	43	29	23	56	23	20	51	31	22	44	23	386
Net inflow (outflow)	20	(4)	(6)	(5)	(29)	14	9	(17)	(8)	7	(10)	12	(17)
OPENING BALANCE (overdraft)	(80)	(60)	(64)	(70)	(75)	(104)	(90)	(81)	(98)	(106)	(99)	(109)	(80)
CLOSING BALANCE (overdraft)	(60)	(64)	(70)	(75)	(104)	(90)	(81)	(98)	(106)	(99)	(109)	(97)	(97)

Appendix 3.2

Notes on Preparation of Cash Flow Forecast

The detailed mechanics of preparing a cash forecast of which an example is shown in Appendix 3.1 can be quite complex and are outside the scope of this work. The following notes therefore deal with the broad principles.

1. The income forecast will be derived from the firm's fee or commission budget. Each month's fees rendered must be spread according to the firm's experience of what proportion of a given month's fees are collected in that and in subsequent months. VAT must be added.

2. The payroll costs should be split between net pay and PAYE and National Insurance.

3. VAT will be derived from the relevant elements of fee income and other expenses (including capital expenditure). Salaries, rent and rates are exempt.

4. Other expenses can conveniently be split between those which accrue more or less evenly during the year and those which fall erratically. The total of each main category of expense should be based on the budget.

5. Partners' drawings should be analysed between monthly payments (which, in all but exceptional circumstances, will inevitably be payable) and special drawings which may be subject to some degree of discretion.

Appendix 3.5 represents the closing balance sheet prepared to confirm the reasonableness of forecasts. Appendix 3.6 show how such a balance sheet is constructed.

Appendix 3.3

Forecast Partnership Profit and Loss Account

Year to 30 April 1987

	£000's	£000's
INCOME		
Fees rendered		319
Increase (decrease) in work in progress		7
		326
*Sundry income and interest received (net)		17
		343
EXPENDITURE		
*Employee costs	152	
*Establishment costs	52	
*Office expenses	49	
*Financial expenses ⎫		
*Other costs ⎬	23	
	—	
		276
NET PRACTISING PROFIT		67

*Supported by subsidiary analyses as appropriate

Appendix 3.4

Fixed Assets Forecast at 30 April 1987

	Cars	Fixtures & fittings	TOTAL
	£	£	£
Cost brought forward	20	10	30
Additions	6	17	23
Cost carried forward	26	27	53
Depreciation brought forward	7	7	14
Disposals	–	–	–
Charge for year	6	3	9
Depreciation carried forward	13	10	23
Net book value carried forward	13	17	30

Depreciation rates:
Cars   25%
Fixtures and fittings   10%

Appendix 3.5

Partnership Balance Sheet 30 April 1987

		Forecast 1987		Actual 1986
PARTNERS' FUNDS AND TAX RESERVES				
		£000's		£
Capital accounts		40		40,000
Current accounts		84		79,893
		124		119,893
Taxation reserves		28		26,100
FUNDS EMPLOYED		152		145,993
EMPLOYMENT OF FUNDS				
FIXED ASSETS		30		16,463
CURRENT ASSETS				
Work in progress	209		201,919	
Client debtors	115		103,834	
Disbursements	22		21,503	
Other debtors	6		4,310	
Bank balance and cash	—		49,095	
	352		380,661	
CURRENT LIABILITIES (excluding taxation)				
Creditors and accruals	133		121,875	
Bank overdraft (net)	97		129,256	
	230		251,131	
NET CURRENT ASSETS		122		129,530
		152		145,993

Appendix 3.6

Working Schedule for Preparation of Forecast Balance Sheet

	Actual balance sheet 30.4.86 £000's	Cash flow movements (Appendix 2.2) £000's	Budgeted profit and loss account year ending 30.4.87 (Appendix 3.1) £000's	Forecast balance sheet 30.4.87 (Appendix 3.3) £000's
Fixed assets	16	23	(9)	30
Current assets				
Work in Progress	202		7	209
Client debtors and W.I.P.	104	(354)	367	117
Other debtors	26	(15)	17	28
	332			354
Current liabilities				
Creditors and Accruals	122	(302)	315	135
Bank overdraft (net)	80	17		97
	202			232
Net current assets	130			122
	146			152
Partners' accounts				
Capital accounts	40			40
Current accounts	80	(43)	47	84
Tax reserves	26	(18)	20*	28
	146			152

* Estimated at average rate for partners

Appendix 3.7 contains brief notes on workings to achieve the forecast closing balance sheet.

Appendix 3.7

Notes on Preparation of Forecast Closing Balance Sheet at 30 April 1987

The forecast balance sheet is derived from three sources:

—the closing balance sheet for the previous year (Appendix 2.2) although where forecasts are being prepared before the new year commences then that balance sheet may also need to be estimated, albeit for only one or two months ahead;
—the budgeted profit and loss account (Appendix 3.3);
—the cash flow forecast (Appendix 3.1).

The working schedule in Appendix 3.6 shows how figures are extracted from each of these sources and used to compile the closing balance sheet.

Cash flow movements are taken inclusive of VAT because the related debtors and creditors are included in the opening balance sheet inclusive of VAT. The total of cash inflows and outflows should equal the net movement in the bank balance, in this case of £17,000.

The profit and loss account includes all figures net of VAT. In order to arrive at the correct figures for debtors and creditors, fees rendered will need to be recalculated with VAT ($319 \times 115/100 = 367$). Expenditure may be divided between that which suffers VAT and that which is zero rated or exempt (salaries, rent and rates are usually the main items) so that VAT can be calculated on relevant expenditure. However, as there will be a net VAT creditor for the difference between VAT amounts charged on income and expenditure, the amount by which fees rendered is increased can simply be added to the movement in expenditure. The figure for expenditure is calculated as follows:

Profit and loss expenditure	276
Depreciation (shown separately)	(9)
VAT paid or payable (367–319)	48
	315

Taxation relating to the profit for the year can be estimated using an average rate for partners. In this case the tax charge of £20,000 is represented by £67,000 at a rate of 30 per cent.

APPENDIX 4
MANAGEMENT REPORTS

Appendix 4.1

Partnership Reporting — An Overview

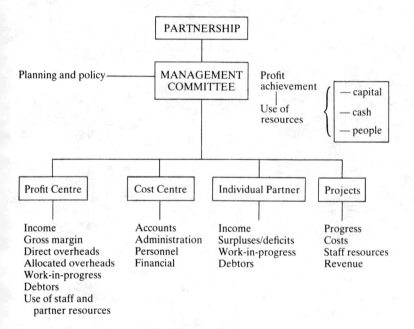

Appendix 4.2

PROFIT CENTRE REPORT

SUMMARY

CENTRE
CIRCULATION:

Prepared by:
Date:
PERIOD:

	THIS PERIOD			YEAR TO DATE		
	ACTUAL	VARIANCE FROM BUDGET		ACTUAL	VARIANCE FROM BUDGET	
	£	£	%	£	£	%
Fees Issued						
Less: Disbursements						
Professional direct costs						
GROSS MARGIN						

Less:

Indirect professional costs

Support staff costs

Accommodation costs

Communication costs

Utilities costs

Other indirect costs

TOTAL INDIRECT COST

NET PRACTISING PROFIT

Appendix 4.3

COST CENTRE REPORT

CENTRE:

CIRCULATION:

Prepared by:

Date:

PERIOD:

| | THIS PERIOD | | | | YEAR TO DATE | |
| | ACTUAL | VARIANCE FROM BUDGET | | | ACTUAL | VARIANCE FROM BUDGET |
	£	£	%		£	£	%
Direct costs							
Salaries							
NI/Pensions							
Staff benefits							
Travel							
Temporary staff							
Equipment & rental							
Equipment maintenance							
Disc storage							
Depreciation							
Consultancy							

	THIS PERIOD £		ACTUAL TO DATE		FORECAST TO COMPLETION	BUDGET £
Direct Expenditure						
Printing & stationery						
Miscellaneous						
Total direct costs						
Attributable Costs						
Accommodation						
Communications						
Utilities						
Total Cost Centre Costs						
Less:						
Recharges to Profit Centres						
Recharge to Projects						
Net Cost Centre Costs						

Appendix 4.4

RESPONSIBLE DEPT:
CIRCULATION

Prepared by:
Date:

PROJECT CONTROL REPORT

PROJECT _____ AS AT _____

	ACTUAL		FORECAST	BUDGET
	THIS PERIOD	TO DATE	TO COMPLETION	
	£	£	£	£

Direct Expenditure

o
o
o
o
o
o

○
○
○
○
Total
Internal Charges
Computer ○
○
○
○
○
Professional ○
○
Other ○
○
Total
Project Total

Appendix 4.5

CIRCULATION

KEY STATISTICS
PERFORMANCE SUMMARY

Prepared by:
Date:
Quarter ended: ......

	THIS QUARTER	YEAR TO DATE	
	ACTUAL	ACTUAL	BUDGET
% return on net capital employed			
Operating profit as % of fees charged			
Cost ratios as % of fee charged			
Number of staff — professional / administration			
Salary costs			
Chargeable time as % of total time available			
Unallocated time as % of total time available			
Other non-chargeable time as % of total time available			
Fees rendered per fee earner			
Total costs per fee earner or per hour fee'd			
Value per hour of time fee'd			

Ratio of current assets to current liabilities			
Work-in-progress (hours and value)			
Estimated number of weeks' work in hand			
Debtors			
Number of weeks' debtors outstanding (at current level of fees)			
Amount of debtors exceeding 90 days			
Number of enquiries — received — converted			
Others			

Index